1

This book belongs to:

_____

Virgo Daily Horoscope 2024

Contents

2024

January

S	M	T	W	T	F	S
	1	2	3	4	5	6
7	8	9	10	11	12	13
14	15	16	17	18	19	20
21	22	23	24	25	26	27
28	29	30	31			

February

S	M	T	W	T	F	S
				1	2	3
4	5	6	7	8	9	10
11	12	13	14	15	16	17
18	19	20	21	22	23	24
25	26	27	28	29		

March

S	M	T	W	T	F	S
					1	2
3	4	5	6	7	8	9
10	11	12	13	14	15	16
17	18	19	20	21	22	23
24	25	26	27	28	29	30
31						

April

S	M	T	W	T	F	S
	1	2	3	4	5	6
7	8	9	10	11	12	13
14	15	16	17	18	19	20
21	22	23	24	25	26	27
28	29	30				

May

S	M	T	W	T	F	S
			1	2	3	4
5	6	7	8	9	10	11
12	13	14	15	16	17	18
19	20	21	22	23	24	25
26	27	28	29	30	31	

June

S	M	T	W	T	F	S
						1
2	3	4	5	6	7	8
9	10	11	12	13	14	15
16	17	18	19	20	21	22
23	24	25	26	27	28	29
30						

July

S	M	T	W	T	F	S
	1	2	3	4	5	6
7	8	9	10	11	12	13
14	15	16	17	18	19	20
21	22	23	24	25	26	27
28	29	30	31			

August

S	M	T	W	T	F	S
				1	2	3
4	5	6	7	8	9	10
11	12	13	14	15	16	17
18	19	20	21	22	23	24
25	26	27	28	29	30	31

September

S	M	T	W	T	F	S
1	2	3	4	5	6	7
8	9	10	11	12	13	14
15	16	17	18	19	20	21
22	23	24	25	26	27	28
29	30					

October

S	M	T	W	T	F	S
		1	2	3	4	5
6	7	8	9	10	11	12
13	14	15	16	17	18	19
20	21	22	23	24	25	26
27	28	29	30	31		

November

S	M	T	W	T	F	S
					1	2
3	4	5	6	7	8	9
10	11	12	13	14	15	16
17	18	19	20	21	22	23
24	25	26	27	28	29	30

December

S	M	T	W	T	F	S
1	2	3	4	5	6	7
8	9	10	11	12	13	14
15	16	17	18	19	20	21
22	23	24	25	26	27	28
29	30	31				

2025

January

S	M	T	W	T	F	S
			1	2	3	4
5	6	7	8	9	10	11
12	13	14	15	16	17	18
19	20	21	22	23	24	25
26	27	28	29	30	31	

February

S	M	T	W	T	F	S
						1
2	3	4	5	6	7	8
9	10	11	12	13	14	15
16	17	18	19	20	21	22
23	24	25	26	27	28	

March

S	M	T	W	T	F	S
						1
2	3	4	5	6	7	8
9	10	11	12	13	14	15
16	17	18	19	20	21	22
23	24	25	26	27	28	29
30	31					

April

S	M	T	W	T	F	S
		1	2	3	4	5
6	7	8	9	10	11	12
13	14	15	16	17	18	19
20	21	22	23	24	25	26
27	28	29	30			

May

S	M	T	W	T	F	S
				1	2	3
4	5	6	7	8	9	10
11	12	13	14	15	16	17
18	19	20	21	22	23	24
25	26	27	28	29	30	31

June

S	M	T	W	T	F	S
1	2	3	4	5	6	7
8	9	10	11	12	13	14
15	16	17	18	19	20	21
22	23	24	25	26	27	28
29	30					

July

S	M	T	W	T	F	S
		1	2	3	4	5
6	7	8	9	10	11	12
13	14	15	16	17	18	19
20	21	22	23	24	25	26
27	28	29	30	31		

August

S	M	T	W	T	F	S
					1	2
3	4	5	6	7	8	9
10	11	12	13	14	15	16
17	18	19	20	21	22	23
24	25	26	27	28	29	30
31						

September

S	M	T	W	T	F	S
	1	2	3	4	5	6
7	8	9	10	11	12	13
14	15	16	17	18	19	20
21	22	23	24	25	26	27
28	29	30				

October

S	M	T	W	T	F	S
			1	2	3	4
5	6	7	8	9	10	11
12	13	14	15	16	17	18
19	20	21	22	23	24	25
26	27	28	29	30	31	

November

S	M	T	W	T	F	S
						1
2	3	4	5	6	7	8
9	10	11	12	13	14	15
16	17	18	19	20	21	22
23	24	25	26	27	28	29
30						

December

S	M	T	W	T	F	S
	1	2	3	4	5	6
7	8	9	10	11	12	13
14	15	16	17	18	19	20
21	22	23	24	25	26	27
28	29	30	31			

2024
Daily Horoscope

VIRGO

"Astrology is a Language. If you understand this language, The Sky Speaks to You."
—*Dane Rudhyar*

JANUARY

Sun	Mon	Tue	Wed	Thu	Fri	Sat
	1	2	3	4	5	6
7	8	9	10	11	12	13
14	15	16	17	18	19	20
21	22	23	24	25	26	27
28	29	30	31			

NEW MOON

WOLF MOON

January

1 Monday

New possibilities kick off a time of sunshine and sparkle, which brings celebration into your life. It promotes stimulating conversations in a social environment that feel good for your soul. It brings a cycle that heralds a new beginning. It brings an active and social time for sharing thoughts and ideas as you network and link up with people who understand your take on life. A situation you invest time and energy into developing blossoms into an enchanting chapter ahead.

2 Tuesday

The planet Mercury turns direct, and this positive cosmic change highlights expansion around your social life. Life heads towards an upswing, bringing an environment ripe with possibility. Clear skies overhead promote a sunny aspect that cultivates friendships and social engagement. Sharing thoughtful discussions bring a happy viewpoint that supports growth in your life. A changing scene on the horizon leaves you feeling optimistic about future possibilities.

3 Wednesday

Being open to new possibilities brings excitement as you discover a journey that speaks to your heart. It rules a time of advancing life towards rising prospects. It offers a social aspect that brings new characters into your life who provide connection and support. As you plug into a journey that aligns with destiny, you feel more in tune with the path forward for your world. It offers a time of lively conversations that focus on entertaining and relaxing with friends.

4 Thursday

The planet Mars sets up camp in Capricorn, and this planetary alignment creates a stable foundation to develop your working goals. Increasing drive attracts an ambitious focus to help you meet the challenges as you build your career path. Capricorn lends more security to the process of developing your goals. It enables you to create tangible progress by developing a stable blueprint for future growth.

5 Friday

Surprise communication paves the way for a reconnection with someone who has been out of the loop. Catching up on the news with this person brings supportive and balanced energy into your life. It has you feeling optimistic about the future as prospects rise and opportunities to socialize link you with a brighter chapter. It enables you to move forward towards an inspiring time of developing personal bonds.

6 Saturday

News arrives, which is a catalyst for expansion in your circle of friends. An emphasis on networking and mingling with friends rekindles growth as you advance life forward. An uptick of social invitations ahead brings fantastic potential into your life as you explore new pathways and get busy growing friendships with kindred spirits. Sharing thoughtful discussions replenishes emotional tanks and promotes happiness.

7 Sunday

Manifesting happiness is on the agenda as a lighter approach draws sunny skies overhead. You share outings with valued companions as you blaze a trail toward a happy and supportive journey. It cracks open a journey of kinship and companionship that bodes well for future goals. Riding a wave of creativity brings epiphanies that help you capture unique possibilities. It gets a chance to rebrand your image and network with others who offer collaboration.

8 Monday

Researching options and planning for future growth helps you move forward with conviction with a correct approach. You trigger a journey of expanding opportunities by being open to progressing your skills and developing your talents. A sense of possibility drives your vision as you chart a course toward developing new leads. Designing the way ahead offers a bright and optimistic fresh start. It sets up a stable foundation that helps progress your situation outwardly.

9 Tuesday ~

Mercury Square Neptune brings new insight into your life. Imagination rises, providing unique ideas and heightened problem-solving abilities. You can reflect on your progress and see you have achieved significant milestones. There will be much to look forward to over the coming months as new possibilities light an optimistic path ahead. Designing goals that link with your abilities helps you chart a course toward an inviting destination.

10 Wednesday

The Mars sextile Saturn aspect brings drive and energy to your daily tasks. Your powers of endurance heighten, enabling you to deal with all the activities on your plate and still have excess energy to burn. Being diligent establishes a stable foundation that lights a path of growth around your life. You discover unique areas that encourage expansion. Sifting and sorting thoughts helps you refine and blend the potential into a unique approach.

11 Thursday

Today, a New Moon offers the chance to plan goals and create a blueprint for future growth. The new possibilities help you set sail on a promise-filled journey. You snag a choice opportunity that brings an upgrade into your life. Being open to change marks a significant turning point that sees rising prospects skyrocket in your situation. It stirs up exciting options that create a gateway toward advancement. A lot of newnesses are coming into your life to keep things exciting.

12 Friday

The Mars trine Jupiter aspect brings a boost to your spirits. It offers a favorable influence that puts the wind back in your sails. Communication arrives that sees improvement occurring in your social life. It opens a prosperous time for social connection, and mingling with friends boosts your spirit. It creates the perfect environment for stepping out into a community setting as you kick-start an active and engaging journey ahead.

13 Saturday

You receive an invitation that lets your social life head on an upswing. As you light up pathways of connectedness and social engagement, you open the gate to refreshing possibilities that draw lighter energy into your life. You enter a cycle of increasing happiness that brings radiance your way. News worth celebrating lands on your doorstep, putting you in a mood to mingle with friends and enjoy companionship.

14 Sunday

Mercury enters your 5th house of creativity, children, and leisure. It's the right vibe to channel your inner child and unlock those parts of yourself buried below the surface. Making time for pleasure and recreation is ideal during this phase. Soul-expanding conversations add a reflective element that offers wisdom and grace. It opens the floodgates to a happy time that emphasizes developing social ties. It gets a chance to unwind with kindred folk in an ambient, engaging environment.

15 Monday

Good news arrives with excitement and opens a positive trend in your life. It is a surprise that carries a bonus that boosts your mood and emphasizes expansion in your social circle. An enriching time shared with friends and companions hits a sweet note in your life's orchestra. It blossoms into a thriving time of sharing thoughtful discussions and entertaining thoughts with others as you grow your world and widen your circle of friends.

16 Tuesday

It is a time that carries you towards a lighter foundation. It does bring positive possibilities that have a substantial impact on improving the journey ahead in your life. Developing your goals and designing projects that inspire and delight help you put the finishing touches on your plans. Improvement overhead marks an essential new beginning that ushers in fresh possibilities. Life revs up with renewed options, and this helps you open up new opportunities.

17 Wednesday

Listening to your emotions taps into the correct path. It lets you show your talents to a broader audience and has you exploring new pathways of growth and prosperity. As you transition towards a positive chapter that expands your horizons into new areas, fortune shines upon your life. News arrives that brings balance and harmony into your life. A fortunate trend comes that blends beautifully with your aspirations for future growth.

18 Thursday

As your priorities shift and change, your situation evolves and reaches new possibilities. It governs a time of increasing potential that helps you turn away from areas that no longer inspire or motivate your spirit. Pouring your energy into growing your passions brings the kind of change that offers forward momentum. It marks a bold beginning that brings greater joy your way—investing time in designing plans and developing projects links to positive change.

19 Friday

Venus faces Neptune in a square that encourages you to look at your romantic goals. You may be seeking something out of reach in your love life. Looking at the filters you have in your love life helps dispel myths and fantasies. Unfulfilled sexual desires may intertwine with unrealistic fanciful expectations and conspire to build an area of denial. This planetary aspect encourages you to take down the castles in the sky and plant your feet in terra firma.

20 Saturday

Today's Sun conjunct Pluto transit increases your power and ability to influence beneficial outcomes. Pluto sets up camp in Aquarius for the next 20 years. It brings the age of Pluto to Aquarius, a time of rising discoveries and scientific exploration. It will emphasize freedom-seeking and new ways of thinking, and this energy promotes developing creative approaches that heighten the potential. It is a welcome paradigm shift that offers to change the world.

21 Sunday

Changes ahead draw significant happenings around your social life. Life attracts a new array of possibilities. Friends seek you out; social engagement is on the rise. It connects the dots in an engaging and happy environment. It opens a serendipitous pathway that fuels well-being as you share thoughts and ideas with friends and family. It promotes news and information and is a welcome remedy for restless energy as you discover new adventures calling for your life.

22 Monday

The path ahead clears and reveals a new landscape of possibility. It allows you to improve your circumstances by expanding life into new areas. Essential changes capture the essence of wanderlust as you head toward unique adventures in your life. Creativity is rising, bringing newfound energy and a burst of inspiration that helps you gain traction on developing impressive goals. As you make progress, you take a positive step toward advancement.

23 Tuesday

Venus settles into Capricorn to heighten security in your life. You have a lot of creativity within your heart that seeks expression in your life. Focusing on developing your talents links you with others who support and nurture your life. The power of inspiration stimulates creative inclinations, drawing new possibilities into your world. Working with your abilities lets you manifest a rewarding result that takes your skills to a higher level of growth.

24 Wednesday

Creating space to nurture abilities brings a unique landscape that promotes creativity. You discover a pathway that captures the essence of inspiration as your imagination dreams up refreshing possibilities that become a source of happiness as you attract positive results. It leads to a journey that progresses skills and elevates prospects around your career. Developments ahead allow pieces of the puzzle to fall into place, creating a bigger picture.

25 Thursday

The Full Moon is a chance to unwind and turn inward as healing, and therapeutically helpful influences wash over your awareness. Being receptive to the Moon's healing qualities offers room to resolve any sensitive areas clinging to your spirit. It propels you towards a journey of promise and healing. Being open to change and expanding your life into new areas creates a slipstream of potential that moves you towards ever-increasing possibilities.

26 Friday

An emphasis on improving your situation brings a curious journey of new horizons. Life keeps the fires of motivation burning as you mingle with kindred spirits and achieve expansion in your social life. It helps you lay stable foundations that provide security, comfort, and growth. Meaningful conversations draw happiness and connection. It opens a unique and original journey that feels the right fit for your life. It improves bonds, promoting a happy time with friends.

27 Saturday

Today, the Sun square Jupiter aspect draws golden vibrations into your life. It raises confidence and leaves you feeling optimistic about your future potential. A more social environment ahead hits the right note for your love life. It stirs the energy of manifestation as you get busy advancing life forward. It shines a light on an expansive and optimistic time that promotes romance in your love life. Sharing brings meaningful moments that grow a bond worth your time.

28 Sunday

The Venus sextile Saturn transit today harmonizes personal bonds. It brings a levelheaded quality to your day-to-day interactions, promoting connection and balance. A new opportunity ahead helps you reach a brighter chapter. It marks a transition that hints at better days. This more encouraging aspect lets you chart a course towards developing meaningful areas around your life. Surging optimism ahead enables you to step out on a journey that holds meaning and promise.

February

Sun	Mon	Tue	Wed	Thu	Fri	Sat
				1	2	3
4	5	6	7	8	9	10
11	12	13	14	15	16	17
18	19	20	21	22	23	24
25	26	27	28	29		

NEW MOON

SNOW MOON

29 Monday

Today's Venus trine Jupiter aspect draws beneficial outcomes into your social and personal life. Singles attract lively possibilities as they resonate with charm and magnetism. A lucky trine adds a dash of spontaneity to your life. It speaks of a turning point that offers advancement for your life. Sunnier skies bring a lighter element into your world. This expansion cycle leads to a breakthrough that brings social engagement and happiness.

30 Tuesday

Many new options ahead help you turn a corner and grow a path that expands life outwardly. Growth and discovery are vital elements that lighten the way forward. Creativity and inspiration flow freely into your world as you hone in on your true purpose. The energy of manifestation draws a cycle of growth and opportunity into your world. It lets you score a significant victory by effectively channeling your energy into a worthwhile area.

31 Wednesday

A positive influence ahead that helps you craft your vision for future growth and journey towards advancing life. Creativity soars under a positive effect that cultivates a unique landscape. It brings a productive and energetic time where significant change leads life forward. Positive news emerges and shines a light on the possible when you expand your vision. It helps build a stable foundation in your life. It is fertile ground for creativity, bringing a winning chapter into view.

1 Thursday

New options draw creativity and inspiration into your world as you hone in on refining your talents and working with your abilities to bring a bumper crop of potential to your door. An emphasis on growth taps into a manifestation pathway. It draws a cycle of opportunity that scores good fortune. Necessary changes ahead see you gain new friends and circulate with valued companions. It brings more communication and potential flowing into your social life.

2 Friday

Today, intuition sparks under the Mercury sextile with Neptune. You may feel more sensitive under this cosmic influence. Still, it also increases communitive abilities, which helps you dig deeper and gain information below the surface of words and gestures. You have undergone many changes recently, leaving you feeling out of sorts. Taking a break from everyday routines and engaging in activities that connect with friends draws lighter energy into your life.

3 Saturday

Being open to change draws a pleasing result for your life. Weeding out areas that limit progress helps you achieve a beautiful shift forward. It brings headway around developing your love life. This progression lets you dive into a refreshing aspect that ignites the more significant potential in your world. A slow and steady approach offers a landscape of possibility. It brings thoughtful and engaging conversations that grow a bond.

4 Sunday

Mercury ingress Aquarius has you seeking answers in your life; hot on the tail of this transit is Mercury conjunct Pluto, which adds intensity to personal communication. Probing questions reveal hidden answers today. It can feel unsettling; pausing and reflecting help nurture balanced foundations. Some positive news is looming overhead as it brings a supportive environment shared with friends.

5 Monday

You develop innovative solutions that offer new flavors. An area you become involved with developing takes on great importance in your life. It brings a busy time to progress your dreams, creating a positive shift that releases the pressure. It stabilizes foundations and brings much-needed downtime. Moving past the barriers, you discover a landscape ripe with possibility. It gets more outstanding balance and stability into your world, which offers an essential upgrade.

6 Tuesday

You open a new chapter in your book of life and discover a vast landscape of possibility that is tempting you forward. Nurturing your creativity stirs up exciting options. You peel back the layers and reveal latent abilities ready for refinement as you grow and evolve. Things are ready to shift forward as a new opportunity lets you channel your energy productively and efficiently. You head towards growth, bringing options that are right for progression.

7 Wednesday

Broadening your horizons lets you explore leads that offer room to build upon your skills. It reawakens a rich landscape of potential as you crack the code that nurtures your talents. Indeed, rising potency and manifestation create an enriching chapter that sets the tone for developing stable foundations. Curious changes draw an enterprising path that becomes a significant turning point in your life.

8 Thursday

The Mars sextile with Neptune today raises charisma and increases your appeal to others. This planetary aspect improves confidence as you radiate charm and find social interactions easy and flowing. The future looks rosy as you deepen a bond and land in an exciting landscape that draws romance and magic into your life. A buzz of activity ahead attracts romance and thoughtful discussions. Meaningful gestures set the tone for developing stable foundations.

9 Friday

You receive news and an invitation that brings a social vibe to light. It places you in contact with kindred spirits who offer lively discussions and dialogues. You usher in a time of happiness as opportunities to mingle arise out of the blue. A spontaneous element lights up pathways that offer lightness and prosperity. It brings a perfect time to cook up a storm and share a journey of social engagement with friends.

10 Saturday

Mercury Square Jupiter adds distraction which brings a lapse of concentration. You may find it challenging to follow conversations and stay on track as your mind tends to wander under this planetary aspect. Creating a distraction-free plan can enable you to limit issues under this dreamy transit. If that feels too challenging, positively harness this energy by jotting down your dreams and goals for future development. Working with planetary energy is always helpful.

11 Sunday

Being receptive to change sparks your creativity and attracts unique options. Something around the corner brings a burst of inspiration that motivates you to grow your abilities and head towards individual pathways that offer growth and improvement. Nurturing your life provides an enriching journey that builds stable foundations and attracts well-being and happiness into your life. You open your world up to new adventures that let you set sail toward developing your dreams.

12 Monday

Events ahead carry you forward as they form a favorable window of opportunity in your life. A fresh cycle beckons, bringing exciting developments that encourage you to grow your world. Being open to new possibilities lets you create headway on improving the building blocks of your life. It ramps up new options and links you with a trajectory that offers growth and progress. It helps you break fresh ground as new possibilities come knocking.

13 Tuesday

Mars ingress Aquarius brings forward-thinking ideas that revolutionize the potential possible in your world. The Venus sextile Neptune brings a sense of anticipation into your life that has you looking forward to Valentine's Day. It offers big-sky dreaming as you indulge in romantic fantasies. It draws a warm and enchanting journey for your romantic life. Nurturing your life draws dividends as it brings a meaningful shift forward that opens a path toward exciting adventures.

14 Wednesday

Mars conjunct Pluto brings the drive and passion to your goals. It heightens sexual drive and desires, helping you nail your romantic goals today. News arrives that brings excitement and possibility. This information opens a new page for your love life as you spotlight an engaging time that brings goodness into your world. Overall, the landscape ahead is transforming, and keeping open to deepening romance lets you obtain growth and progress.

15 Thursday

Surprise news leads to an invitation out and about. It brings a social aspect that offers a lively environment. It helps you build secure and stable foundations as new possibilities flow in and tempt you forward. A rise in confidence helps expand life. Socializing with your broader circle of friends delivers abundance into your world. It emphasizes nurturing supportive conversations and sharing with companions. Getting involved with a social group draws well-being and harmony.

16 Friday

Venus sashays into Aquarius to raise the vibration in your romantic life. It showers harmonious beams over your social world, contributing to rising prospects in your life. Your life heads to an upswing as social invitations bring a flurry of engagement into view. It offers a journey that aligns with developing personal bonds. Spending time with kindred spirits brings lively discussions, and you discover life becoming sweeter and lighter.

17 Saturday

Unwrapping the way ahead brings a pleasant surprise that promotes happiness. You discover several opportunities swirling around your social life that tempt you towards growing your world outwardly. It brings a lively and dynamic environment that offers activities and sharing with friends. Lively discussions ensure bright ideas grow your creativity and bring new projects and endeavors to the surface.

18 Sunday

The conditions are perfect for sharing and embracing a time of relaxation and rejuvenation. News arrives that brings sweet notes into your social life. Engaging with a broader world of potential sees companionship flourish as new ideas and possibilities crop up. It brings a motivational time to invest energy into your social life. Connecting with your tribe brings fresh ideas and inspiration to the forefront of your life.

19 Monday

Several opportunities are swirling around your social life, tempting you to share thoughts with others. It brings a lively environment that offers activities and sharing with friends. You sail on a voyage that brings joy and harmony into your life. It puts a focus on freedom, abundance, and manifestation. It offers a luminescent journey that aligns with your dreams. It lifts the lid on an enterprising chapter that draws stability to your world.

20 Tuesday

You hit the road running and soon advance towards an inspiring time of increasing your skills and taking in new areas for development. It marks a bold beginning transforming life as you build stable foundations that offer progression. Effective changes open up a more prosperous path forward. Creating space to nurture your talents draws an optimistic shift that carries you on a journey that marks a significant turning point in your life.

21 Wednesday

You soon hit your stride in a new chapter of growth. Removing the heaviness and pushing back the barriers brings a lighter chapter that nurtures your abilities and grows your talents. It translates to new energy that encourages the continuation of a theme representing transformation. Riding a wave of good power opens the floodgates to new possibilities. A unique path calls your name, as expanding horizons offers a light aspect that draws fruitful results.

22 Thursday

Venus conjunct Mars increases sexual charisma and drive. It heightens intimacy and yearning for exceptional bonding. If you crave romantic downtime today, you know which planets are involved in the passion propelling you toward creating magic in your love life. You find peace by creating a sanctuary around your romantic life. It plants the seeds that draw stability and balance into your immediate environment.

23 Friday

Thanks to Mercury slipping into Pisces to increase your thought processes, you receive a boost of mental clarity and an uptick in analytical reasoning abilities today. It enables you to stretch past your comfort zone and discover new possibilities that offer transformation. A unique option emerges, which gives you a chance to develop your abilities and grow the path ahead. A strong emphasis on evolving your skills lets you capture the essence of advancement.

24 Saturday

A Full moon in Virgo draws understanding, clarity, and insight. It offers a broader overview of your life, nurturing a therapeutic and healing environment. It brings a time of healing the past. You may face an uncertain future, but one thing is for sure, the more you work on the foundations of your life, the better you will be positioned to achieve the best outcome possible. Finding balance and maintaining a middle ground brings more excellent stability.

25 Sunday

Venus Square Jupiter's planetary aspect brings a fun-loving vibe into your social life. Good fortune, sharing, and caring with friends light an engaging path that nurtures well-being and happiness in your life. It takes you on a journey of new horizons which spark movement and discovery. A new approach brings companionship and lively discussions which spark creative ideas. Life soon becomes more expressive and connected.

26 Monday

You enter a new cycle of growth that helps you grow and prosper as you develop your abilities. It links to positive change that lays the groundwork to build a stable foundation in your life. Maintaining excellence draws growth as you receive opportunities that increase your career's potential. It does bring heightened security and a pleasing result to your working goals. A lovely perk arrives, a feather in your cap that has you re-evaluating your working life goals.

27 Tuesday

Mars square Jupiter brings positive energy, heightening confidence and enthusiasm for life. It enables you to progress your vision by connecting you with growth opportunities. Forging ahead and developing your goals helps you accomplish the correct result. Serendipitous changes ahead give you glimmers of possibility, and following this trial draws prosperity. It enables you to craft a blossoming path as you design goals that suit your expertise.

28 Wednesday

Sun conjunct Mercury brings news and communication. As communication tumbles into your world, you see an emerging theme of abundance. It magnifies the potential possible as you transition towards developing personal ties. It brings a colorful chapter that expands your life outwardly with social opportunities. You enter a soul-stirring chapter that lifts the lid on new possibilities. Socialising and networking lead to a get-together with people who boost morale and share ideas.

29 Thursday

Jupiter's positive vibration seals that deal on a Mercury-infused forward-thinking day. Mercury in sextile with Jupiter offers an ideal opportunity to think about the future and brainstorm as you plan future goals. The wheels are in motion to attract incoming opportunities that help grow the path ahead. It creates an engaging chapter for exploring new avenues. Game-changing information arrives that hits an upward trend. It brings room to expand your skills into a unique area.

MARCH

Sun	Mon	Tue	Wed	Thu	Fri	Sat
					1	2
3	4	5	6	7	8	9
10	11	12	13	14	15	16
17	18	19	20	21	22	23
24	25	26	27	28	29	30
31						

VIRGO

New Moon

WORM MOON

MARCH

1 Friday

One of astrology's most favored transits lights up your day. In sextile with Jupiter, the Sun brings golden beams of positivity into your life. It draws freedom and change as you expand your horizons outwardly and embrace a sense of connection with your broader circle of friends. Like-minded people offer engaging discussions and advice. A new cycle arrives, bringing a welcome boost of invitations that inspire social growth.

2 Saturday

You usher in an expressive journey that cultivates lively discussions and social engagement. It shines a light on harmony as you open life to a new landscape. News arrives that promotes blessings as it activates a social environment that brings the opportunity to mingle with engaging companions. It draws lively discussions and carries a uniquely uplifting time that boosts lighter energy. It opens a journey that highlights growth around your friendship circle.

3 Sunday

Venus Square Uranus brings restless energy that offers deliberate you from constraints that keep you tied down and feeling limited. You feel called to liberate yourself from restrictive circumstances and patterns. It brings a spontaneous element that promotes refreshing adventures that change your day-to-day routines. It lays the groundwork for a more connected future as lively discussions bring an enriching chapter to light.

4 Monday

Something percolating in the background of your life will soon appear to point the right path forward. You move forward confidently, and acting on your instincts results in valuable results. Clearing the way the cobwebs offers an open road of potential as you pursue advancing your life into uncharted territory. Transformation sweeps in to encourage expansion and growth. It lifts the barriers that limit progress as you broaden your world by being open to change.

5 Tuesday

Opportunities crop up, which encourages you to dream big. Your intuition guides this process, and you feel drawn to developing a path that reveals hidden depths in your abilities. Immersing yourself in the building blocks gets you back to basics and grounds your energy in a helpful area. It creates a balanced and stable environment from which to nurture your dreams. It culminates in a pathway that promotes well-being and draws abundance into your surroundings.

6 Wednesday

A dream comes into focus, giving you the green light to connect with inspiration and creativity. It draws new pathways that advance your vision forward. It encourages you to push past limitations and expand your horizons into new areas. It means stepping out of your comfort zone and developing regions that come calling to grow your talents. Rising creativity and adaptability help you seize opportunities that come your way.

7 Thursday

Greener pastures beckon, which draws information that inspires rising prospects in your working life. It helps you touch down on a promising journey of evolving your situation. It culminates in a turning point, becoming the catalyst for growing your dreams. Working towards your vision takes this project to a new level. It brings a time of gaining traction and nailing your goals. Something big unfolds in your creative life; working to your plans allows things to come together in time.

8 Friday

You receive an invitation to an event that promotes new adventures in your social life. Life opens to a time of freedom and adventure that promotes developing bonds in your life. Sharing with friends refuel's energy tanks and has you feeling motivated and inspired to expand life. Open communication brings an impressive time of sharing thoughtful dialogues that shines a light on wellness, rejuvenation, and renewal as you enter a happy chapter.

9 Saturday

A Mars square Uranus planetary transit hits a freedom-loving vibe in time for Saturday night adventures. It brings a restlessness that seeks expression as you break free from constraints and head towards a liberating time shared with friends. It heightens emotional well-being and supports your world with thoughtful conversations that bring new possibilities to light. It gives you the green light to chase your dreams and head towards rising prospects in your life.

10 Sunday

Mercury ingress Aries offers improvement as newfound energy and drive help you accomplish a great deal. It helps you plan for future growth by bringing news and information your way. You have been through some challenges but can soon lift the lid on new options that inspire growth in your life. An emphasis on improving your situation draws a pleasing result. It launches a time of developing goals that strongly focus on your family life. Nurturing your home space draws joy.

MARCH

11 Monday

Venus ingress Pisces is a favorable transit for your love life. Life brings essential changes that enable you to embrace a more progressive aspect. It harmonizes emotional bonds and elevates potential in your personal life. It points toward a happy chapter that lets you leave struggles behind in the rear vision mirror. It brings steady progress that boosts interpersonal bonds and family ties. Mingling and networking draw a productive and lively environment.

12 Tuesday

Exploring diverse pathways will drive you toward prosperity if you feel stuck and restlessness comes calling. You can come up with creative solutions to age-old problems. Being open to developing your skills helps you unearth the advancement that takes your talents to the next level. You connect with a journey that opens new pathways and possibilities in your world. Advancing your life into unique areas takes you towards growth and rising prospects.

13 Wednesday

Life brims with excellent options as you create new pathways. An exciting journey ahead fills in the blanks. It starts a new trend that migrates away from difficulties as you make the most of an influx of options that grow your abilities. It puts you on a course to advance your talents and deepen your knowledge. Working effectively and exploring options lets you move toward a successful outcome. It opens up new avenues that take your skills to the next level.

14 Thursday

Events on the horizon trigger growth in your life. It allows you to open a unique path filled with possibilities. Synchronicity guides this journey, creating the right environment for energy to flow easily. You soon develop a project that charts a course to rising prospects. Many new options are coming; it brings a chance to develop artistic talents and take your abilities to the next level. This potential ripens and blossoms into a meaningful journey forward.

15 Friday

A clean slate of potential brings an open road for developing new adventures. It launches creativity higher, enabling you to design plans that offer advancement. Dissolving the outworn areas and releasing the blocks brings new options that touch your life with good fortune. You enter a profitable time of working with your creativity and developing a journey that governs increasing happiness. Learning and growth are at the crux of reaching for your dreams.

16 Saturday

Invitations, news, and engagement carry you forward to greener pastures. It lets you embrace a more connected chapter as you move away from limitations and head toward growth. An active time of mingling brings a unique friendship to light. It offers a joyful time that ignites inspiration and happiness in your life. Focusing on social engagement brings rising prospects into your life. It emphasizes engaging with sharing trailblazing discussions that light up growth pathways.

17 Sunday

Sun conjunct Neptune transit increases intuition and empathy today. It brings an appropriate time to reflect and contemplate future dreams and goals. Something new on offer rewards you with a positive influence. It opens the door to a brighter chapter that grows your life in a meaningful area. It brings lighter energy into your life, which helps shore up any flagging foundations. It offers a prime time to set new goals and plan the path onward.

18 Monday

Advancement comes calling and brings new responsibilities and a learning curve. It does help you achieve remarkable growth as your talents become stronger and influence the trajectory of your vision for future growth. You put your foot forward in a progressive and robust environment by leaning into challenges by utilizing your skills and previously gained wisdom. New assignments bring opportunities for collaboration.

19 Tuesday

New information brings insight into the path ahead. You discover a social environment that promotes friendship and connection. It brings expansion to your circle and facilitates thoughtful discussions that nurture happiness. Your social life hums and brings refreshing and exciting developments that are key to future growth. Emphasizing nurturing personal ties draws an open road of potential. You enter a more abundant landscape when new possibilities inspire change.

20 Wednesday

You reveal that strategizing with kindred spirits rules a time of expansion in your life. It enables you to craft plans that hold water and offer advancement. You attract the correct type of opportunities that elevates your talents and grows your abilities. You discover an atmosphere ripe with possibility that holds a positive influence as it cultivates creativity and inspiration. With motivation running hot, you soon find a breathtaking direction.

21 Thursday

Sun sextile Pluto transit increases your drive. You feel more determined and purposeful than usual, which helps you achieve your goals today. You take disciplined action as you have the drive and perseverance to nail developing your dreams. You charge ahead towards more outstanding achievements by planning the path and setting intentions. Your dedication draws dividends as you pivot away from hurdles and channel your energy into developing an essential objective.

22 Friday

The transit of Mars in Pisces reduces issues in your life as this favorable aspect draws good fortune and rising prospects. It elevates financial possibilities, leading to a winning path forward. Extra activities with your circle of friends sustain your spirit and draw happiness. You can spread your wings and enjoy a lively environment that cultivates thoughtful discussions and fresh ideas. It helps you turn the leaf on a new chapter of life.

23 Saturday

Life comes up with new options for mingling and connecting with friends. It does keep you on your feet as surprise communication flips the switch on a spontaneous adventure. It deepens personal ties and places emphasis on developing bonds. Happy tidings shared in a lively environment foster engaging conversations. Unexpected news brings a joyous celebration that prepares you to engage in growing life.

24 Sunday

Venus sextile Jupiter raises confidence as good fortune flows into your life. It introduces a lucky aspect that improves finances, relationships, and circumstances. Attractive options ahead help you move away from sadness. Thoughtful discussions cultivate rising creativity, leading to new ideas for future development. It helps establish your talents in an area worth your time. It's the perfect time to map out new goals for your life.

25 Monday

A Full Moon brings healing into your surroundings to wash away the outworn areas and soothe your spirit with a therapeutic influence. Personal sacrifice has been too prominent in your life. Making your goals a priority helps dissolve old wounds with an emotional beginning that supports wellness and happiness. It brings a creative element that enables you to develop new projects. An experimental flavor allows you to dabble in hobbies and discover unique areas.

26 Tuesday

You lean into challenges and embrace growing your abilities. Working with your talents helps you close the door on a difficult time, and as the chaos fades from your life, you discover a lucky aspect that draws good fortune. You become involved in using your talents to design and grow a path forward for your life. It offers lighter energy that anchors you to a grounded and secure environment that promotes happiness.

27 Wednesday

Dipping your skills into the pot of potential brings a growth-orientated phase. A focus on advancement elevates your skills and grows your abilities. It sets the right foundations from which to expand your world. Prioritizing your goals helps light creativity and artistic expression pathways. Getting involved with areas that offer growth, learning, and advancement helps build stable foundations which kick-start a new enterprise.

28 Thursday

Taking time to nurture your foundations and focusing on areas that hold meaning in your life draws dividends. You lift the lid on a busy time that helps you gather your resources and prepare for a new chapter of potential. News arrives that brings a piece of sweet information. It offers a considerable boost and hints at a unique journey ahead. New goals build on the foundations you create during this time. It turns the leaf into a new chapter that encourages and motivates change.

29 Friday

You discover a social environment that brings a fresh wind of potential which carries you forward. Circulating with friends helps establish a genuine friendship that twinkles brightly with possibility. Golden threads of magic weave fantastic outcomes around your life as you emphasize developing personal ties. It beautifully reinvigorates your spirit and grows your life in a meaningful direction. It brings a lively time that draws happiness into your world.

30 Saturday

Good fortune slips into your world and brings sharing company to the forefront. Sharing companionship with people who resonate on your wavelength draws happiness. It focuses on developing personal ties and welcoming friends in a warm and engaging environment. You settle into a cozy and cheerful zone that brings time for family and friends. An invitation to a celebratory event brings sparkle and flair to your life.

31 Sunday

Positively directing your energy and channeling efforts into your social life brings a bumper crop of potential. You plant the seeds and come up with roses as you benefit from events on the horizon. Opportunities to mingle emerge from a variety of sources and place emphasis on nurturing social ties. It improves home and family life and offers a remarkable, heartening trajectory for more excellent stability.

APRIL

Sun	Mon	Tue	Wed	Thu	Fri	Sat
	1	2	3	4	5	6
7	8	9	10	11	12	13
14	15	16	17	18	19	20
21	22	23	24	25	26	27
28	29	30				

NEW MOON

Pink Moon

APRIL

1 Monday

Mercury turns Retrograde on April Fools' Day, bringing a little joke from the heavens. It is a time that stalls progress as miscommunication and mixed signals are more prevalent in your social life. Improving the basis of your foundations brings structure and balance. It reawakens creativity and brings growth to the forefront of your life. It offers a soothing element that balances frazzled nerves and harmonizes your spirit during this challenging planetary aspect.

2 Tuesday

It is a fruitful time that attracts opportunities not previously encountered. It begins a path of expanding options that ushers in change. The tides turn in your favor as a lucky break brings increasing opportunities. It offers new beginnings that stir creative inclinations, promoting the development of innovative projects. Tapping into your ability to manifest personal goals creates rising inspiration that provides a flurry of possibility.

3 Wednesday

Venus conjunct Neptune brings rising possibilities for singles to find a romantic partner. It also offers advancement for couples as a favorable influence nurtures growth. Being open to options opens the door to an exciting chapter that stimulates growth and progress. It brings lively discussions and an expansive chapter that feels right for your world. Exploring the synergy with someone caring and attentive governs increasing possibilities for growing love.

4 Thursday

Keeping your energy open helps you achieve growth in your life. Dissolving blocks creates space for new possibilities to flourish. News arrives that sparks a journey of growth, learning, and wisdom. It shines on your abilities and brings an enriching chapter to light. It marks a time of shifting your energy forward as you feed the creativity within and heighten the potential in your world. An enterprising area offers exciting prospects that become part of an extensive chapter of growth.

5 Friday

Venus ingress Aries brings a thoughtful aspect that helps you rediscover your passion and creativity. It places the spotlight on nurturing hobbies and growing interests in your life. It is an incredibly potent time to grow your world as you enter a cycle of increasing options. It places you in an excellent position to achieve tangible results. Setting intentions and maintaining a positive outlook paves the way forward.

6 Saturday

Venus sextile Pluto adds depth, meaning, and curiosity. It has you wanting to peel back the layers and discover what lies beneath the surface of everyday life. Screening out distractions brings depth, purpose, structure, and balance to your life. It brings progress and a new source of prosperity to explore. You are ready to craft your vision and head towards developing your dreams. As you open the book on a new realm of potential, you stir up exciting options worth your time.

7 Sunday

A new approach takes prominence and brings a time of expanding your life outwardly. It brings people into your circle who provide insight, advice, and ideas. Blending the energies with friends brings a new possibility to light. It marks a time of exploring options and getting involved with a group project. It's a journey that draws contentment and joy into your life. It speaks of a shift forward that provides you with an open road of possibility.

8 Monday

You can leverage your skills and gain an advantage over the path ahead. You can create the building blocks that give you a stable platform. Working with your abilities brings an upgrade that nurtures advancement. It brings new opportunities to explore, grow, and deepen your talents. You unwrap a chapter that holds unique possibilities and brings growth to your life. As you lay the groundwork for the path ahead, you enter a productive and progressive time.

9 Tuesday

Your creativity brings a shift in understanding that guides the path. It helps you reach a pinnacle point in your career path that spells advancement. Opportunity comes knocking as curious changes ahead bring an improvement of circumstances to your door. It ushers in a time of refreshing possibilities that helps you make strides in advancing your goals. It connects you with a phase of expansion that offers rising prospects that help you chart a course forward.

10 Wednesday

Mars conjunct Saturn ignites determination and drive, which helps you excel in the workplace. Your career heads towards advancement and takes you on a journey that deepens your knowledge. News ahead lights an exciting path forward for your working life. It gives you the green light to get involved with an endeavor that opens a fortunate trend for your career path. Setting your sights on achieving growth brings a time of progress and advancement.

11 Thursday

You attract excellent possibilities that add value to your life. Working efficiently, you advance towards an attractive option. It brings a golden area that paves the way forward. An assignment crops up that seems a good fit for your abilities. It brings a decision and changes as you climb the ladder toward success. It emphasizes developing your working life as you find new challenges to sink your teeth into producing.

12 Friday

Dabbling in your interests shines a light on growing a creative enterprise. Working with your talents draws a nurturing influence that releases outworn areas and builds stable foundations that rebalance and rejuvenate your life. It soon translates to a fresh start that offers rising prospects. It does reveal pathways that deepen your knowledge and develop your talents. You refine your abilities and connect with a vibrant landscape that provides growth and rising prospects.

13 Saturday

Favorable changes draw social opportunities which bring a memorable time into your life. As you head out and embrace a more social environment, life takes on a rosy glow. It plants the seed for a more connected environment as sharing with your tribe gets a welcome boost that nurtures happiness. It connects you with someone who offers engaging advice. It brings an invitation to mingle that leads to soul-stirring discussions and happy trails forward for your social life.

14 Sunday

You face a crossroads, and a decision is required to step past this juncture and head toward your vision. There is a path that speaks to your heart directly. Your intuition guides this process, and you feel it is in the right direction. It does see you heading towards change as you reveal hidden depths of insight that enable progress to occur. Removing the confusion allows for a unique journey to blossom.

15 Monday

Striking while the iron is hot helps put plans into action. You receive an important message that offers a missing puzzle piece. It leads to a meaningful conversation that lets you learn more about an area that had felt incomplete. Clearing outworn energy provides a refreshing landscape that lets you move forward with growth plans. Newfound power propels you forward toward developing your vision. Making the most of this forward momentum helps you manifest your vision.

16 Tuesday

Unexpected opportunities provide a chance to grow your skills. A project crops up that offers more range and depth for your creativity. It provides impressive results that advance your skills and allows you to grow and gain valuable experience. A positive influence offers expansion and gain, improving your life's security. It shifts your emphasis to increasing your life in a direction that promotes a pleasing result.

17 Wednesday

You optimize your circumstances by exploring various avenues of possibility. Investigating unique options brings a steady growth cycle that has you working smarter, not harder. Life settles into a more enriching phase that rewards you with growth. It refuels your emotional tanks and draws support as you deepen the potential possible in your life. Heightened security attracts grounded foundations that strengthen your life.

18 Thursday

A lovely trend ahead promotes expansion in your life. It brings a chance to work with your creativity and move towards rising prospects. It brings a sense of hope and optimism that surges into your world with new projects and activities on the cards. Finding a greater understanding of purpose cracks the code to an enterprising time working with your abilities. The possibilities will be plentiful as new options spark growth.

19 Friday

Mars sextile Jupiter transit makes you feel confident today. This planetary aspect is ideal for tackling complex tasks because there is an excellent chance of success. This transit has a well-earned reputation for good luck as it increases optimism and initiative and brings a willingness to take calculated risks. It gets the chance to rebrand your life and reinvent your talents. Growing your abilities creates ideal conditions to dig deep and reveal latent gifts ready to be refined.

20 Saturday

Mars sextile Uranus offers unique ideas that help you think outside the box to obtain innovative solutions. Uranus places the focus on rebellion, liberation, and freedom. It adds a dash of spontaneity to your life today. You head towards an active time of engaging with your social life. It brings outings and opportunities that feel adventurous. Keeping life vivid and dynamic draws happy times that uplift the mood. You find flavor by adding variety to your life.

21 Sunday

Jupiter's conjunct Uranus transit provides surprises and sudden opportunities. Good news lands in a flurry of excitement. Circulating and mingling attract well-being and harmony, which boosts your morale as you discover a journey filled with progress and happy moments. Nurturing happiness in your life brings an optimistic influence. As you enjoy lighter overtones, you connect with others who offer supportive conversations and mingling opportunities.

22 Monday

Things are ready to turn a corner in your life. New leads emerge that have you thinking about growth, learning, and advancement. A course or other learning possibility is a source of inspiration that helps break down barriers and lead you toward development. It offers both challenges and progression in your life. Being open to possibilities advance life towards greener pastures. It brings a journey of self-development that lets you touch down on an ample time of growing dreams.

23 Tuesday

The Full Moon draws a healing and therapeutic influence into your life. Releasing limiting beliefs moves you toward refreshing options that open a journey ripe for growing. You discover a therapeutic situation for your spirit as it heals old wounds. A richer life experience arrives to heal an aspect that has been out of alignment recently. It does help you release bottled-up emotions that have caused tension that limited your true potential.

24 Wednesday

Tweaking and refining your goals helps create the right approach to launch forward toward your vision. You reveal precious resources at hand that enable you to build plans. It opens the doors to a journey of growing your life. You harness the essence of efficiency to improve your bottom line. It spotlights developing a long-held dream, which brings a richly creative landscape to grow your world. It creates the right environment to explore new avenues of prosperity.

25 Thursday

Mercury turns direct, improving personal bonds and opening the path to growing your social life. It opens an engaging time in your personal life that pushes back the barriers to reveal an exciting way forward. It marks the beginning of an enriching journey that brings rising prospects to your romantic life—sharing thoughtful discussions nurtures grounded foundations that trigger progress and joy.

26 Friday

Positive energy is ready to flow into your life. Nurturing your creativity illuminates new options worth your time and energy. You may feel unsure about the path ahead but growing your life is the surefire ticket to advance toward success. Being open to connecting with people and possibilities helps you rise above the drama and embrace enriching your life. The choices and decisions you make drive expansion. It brings an empowering chapter of growing your world.

27 Saturday

Life becomes a blaze of new potential soon. Events line up to nourish your soul and nurture well-being in your life. Your willingness to work towards your dreams opens up an abundant landscape that lets you create remarkable progress in your world. The way forward becomes bright and optimistic as you get a chance to rejuvenate life and nurture a wellspring of possibility. It offers an opportunity to catch up with friends. Surprise news lights the path forward.

28 Sunday

Involvement with home and family matters offers social engagement and a chance to cultivate meaningful friendships. Communication flows easily, ramping up the potential in your social life. A sweet and productive vibe promotes expansion in your life. It opens the gate to a new chapter that is ripe with possibility. A situation you deepen takes on a life of its own and begins to blossom. A strong emphasis on improving circumstances culminates in a journey offering expansive horizons.

MAY

Sun	Mon	Tue	Wed	Thu	Fri	Sat
			1	2	3	4
5	6	7	8	9	10	11
12	13	14	15	16	17	18
19	20	21	22	23	24	25
26	27	28	29	30	31	

New Moon

FLOWER MOON

----

29 Monday

Venus in Taurus brings a harmonizing influence that offers grounded foundations for your social life. It helps you approach relationships and life warmly, earthy and balanced manner. Today, a Mars conjunct Neptune aspect raises potential in your romantic life; it has you dreaming big about the possibilities. The events ahead offer remarkable opportunities for growth and happiness. It opens an expressive journey that sees you spending time with people you value.

30 Tuesday

Mars lands in Aries, and this raises confidence. It's time to go big and be bold. Your best qualities will enter the spotlight and gain recognition soon. It brings a page-turning chapter when the path ahead clears. Staying flexible lets you chart a course that takes in new prospects. It opens an empowering time for developing your skills and improving the foundations of your life, as pushing back the barriers marks a time of remarkable growth.

1 Wednesday

Today's aspect could see a flare-up of jealousy or possessiveness. Your romantic partner may feel threatened by heightened social activities and invitations flowing into your life. Take time to support and boost confidence to help offset the Venus square Pluto aspect. Being aware of these fears' dynamics helps keep relationships healthy and balanced. You may find it challenging to stay on track with developing personal bonds under this planetary aspect.

2 Thursday

Pluto is the modern ruler of Scorpio; it symbolizes how we experience power, renewal, rebirth, and mysterious or subconscious forces. This Pluto retrograde phase allows you to dive deep and explore inner realms and darker aspects of your personality ordinarily hidden from view. Understanding your psyche deeper provides access to the forces driving your personality. It has you evaluating all aspects of your life as soul-searching brings insights into areas of interest.

3 Friday

Mars sextile Pluto transit increases energy in the workplace. No job is too small as you take on the lot and work towards your vision. Working effectively and efficiently towards your goals hold you in good stead. You no longer feel as though you are treading water; you begin to see the progress you have worked tirelessly to achieve. It opens avenues that encourage expansion. It brings a time of rising prospects for building your dreams and developing your goals.

4 Saturday

News arrives, which brightens the landscape ahead. It lets you create strides in improving the foundations, allowing you to expand the borders and head toward growth. A change of direction brings more incredible blessings into your life. It triggers a positive change that takes your vision further. A pathway opens for your social life; this becomes a strong focus for you moving forward. As you create headway in developing your life, you connect with a happy time.

5 Sunday

New options are arriving in your life soon. It brings a social aspect that offers companionship and friendship. A bustling and active time of sharing thoughts and engaging with your broader circle of friends lifts the lid on developing camaraderie in your life. Much potential surrounds your life, and an expansive phase of moving past perceived barriers cracks the code to a bright chapter ahead. It offers friendships and social activities that draw well-being and happiness.

6 Monday

Advancing life toward new areas facilitates growth as you grow your skills in a unique direction. Doing research and exploring new pathways brings high-level options into your life. Opportunities ahead offer a newfound project that becomes a source of inspiration. It brings rising motivation that opens the way toward growth in your life. It ushers in an impressive social aspect that cultivates lively discussions, engagement, and sharing with insightful companions.

7 Tuesday

Sun sextile Saturn transit lends patience and perseverance; it enables you to gain traction on achieving challenging goals in your life. Curious possibilities ahead ramp up motivation and leave you optimistic about life. It promotes a busy time that sees you gaining traction on developing your life outwardly. Difficulties fade as you rekindle inspiration and turn the corner, heading toward growth. It brings unexpected developments into your life that cracks the code to a brighter chapter.

8 Wednesday

You enter a busy time that brings a noteworthy venture. It offers remarkable improvement as it activates your creative abilities. You spend time discussing this new and essential assignment with friends and kindred spirits. Getting feedback helps you refine and make tweaks around this enterprise. Working out the details with a kindred spirit offers a chance for collaboration. It lets you take advantage of supportive conversations that provide good results.

9 Thursday

You receive an upgrade that leaves you smiling. It helps you move forward with freedom, growth, and expansion. You learn the ropes of a new area that leaves you feeling equipped to take on larger goals. It opens the doors to a specific time of developing your talents as you head towards an upward trend that sees your abilities soar to greater heights. It brings an extra element of luck that helps you attain a lofty goal.

10 Friday

Exploring leads opens to unearthing more wondrous magic, which draws abundance into your life. Igniting the fires of inspiration sees creativity rising. It provides a social aspect that draws communication and the sharing of ideas—engaging in brainstorming sessions with kindred spirits blazes a trail toward a successful result. You step out of your comfort zone and explore uncharted territories as you push past perceived barriers.

11 Saturday

Life picks up speed as you enter a busy and active environment. The energy of manifestation swirls gently around your situation, bringing a vital phase of creativity and renewal. Adapting to change is integral in bringing unique potential into your world. It harmonizes and serves nerves and restores foundations. It does get news that enables you to open your life up. It marks a turning point that has you feeling hopeful and excited about future possibilities.

12 Sunday

You nurture social bonds and upgrade your life with a situation that captures your interest and sparks your curiosity. It inspires your life on many levels. It brings changes that resonate warmly in your world. It encourages a greater sense of security and stability as you can focus on improving personal bonds. It charts a course towards rising prospects in your social life as invitations ahead encourage you to step out and enjoy all that life has to offer.

MAY

13 Monday

A positive influence from the Sun conjunct Uranus planetary aspect brings a boost that sparks new options. It opens a journey that holds blessings and offers to revolutionize the potential possible in your world. The Venus sextile Saturn transit today increases your need for company, and you may yearn to connect with friends. You soon land in a refreshing environment that brings new possibilities to light.

14 Tuesday

Doing research and exploring various pathways brings high-level options to consider. It does promote an active phase of growth and development that lets you tap into your talents and advance your skills into a new area. A new option is in the works for your life, allowing you to set a course on developing a site that offers results. It emphasizes growing your life and improving your circumstances. You accomplish a great deal by focusing on the building blocks of life.

15 Wednesday

Mercury settles into Taurus; your thinking is down to earth, balanced, and grounded. Focusing on building stable foundations in your life leads to a busy time that creates headway around some of your larger goals. You accomplish a great deal and enter a time that merges your dreams with tangible results. You attract positive outcomes by maintaining a positive outlook. Building plans and nurturing your abilities draws prospects that create a gateway towards advancement.

16 Thursday

New information lets you gain traction in developing an exciting goal. A cycle of increasing abundance marks a time of magic and excitement. Life becomes active and progressive. A new area comes calling and draws a path that reflects your current hopes and dreams. It lets you sail on a timely voyage towards growing your abilities and working with your talents. It offers ample time that reinvents potential and brings a transition into your life. It advances your goals outwardly.

MAY

17 Friday

You usher in a time of happy surprises that lights a path forward toward expansion. It brings some thoughtful and engaging conversations that blaze a trail toward improvement. It has the added benefit of dialing down stress and anxiety as it brings grounded foundations that nurture well-being and happiness in your life. It draws fresh air and sunny skies into your environment. It connects you with friends and companions as you unpack a chapter of social engagement.

18 Saturday

Venus teams up with Uranus to add a dash of spontaneity to your social/personal life. Another conjunct occurs between the Sun and Jupiter, adding lightness and momentum to your life. Entertaining discussions ahead, crack the code to expand your social life. It puts you in the proper alignment to form a friendship with someone new. Moving out of your comfort zone encourages growth and progress. It opens the floodgates to socializing with your broader circle of friends.

19 Sunday

Nurturing the foundations in your life draws a balanced and abundant landscape. Focusing on the basics around your home life draws a solid foundation to grow your world. A new approach ahead draws lightness and happiness into your life. It brings a strong uptick of potential for your social life, connecting you with companions who support and nurture your world. Sharing thoughtful discussions facilitates harmony.

20 Monday

The pace and rhythm of life pick up speed as you move forward towards progressing your dreams. Positive change cultivates balanced foundations that nurture well-being, supporting growth in your life. Rising prospects are a prominent theme in your life as you seek further opportunities that promote growth in your world. Progression is imminent as you break fresh ground and gain traction on progressing your dreams.

21 Tuesday

An opportunity emerges that connects with your long-term vision for your career path. Polishing your expertise and developing your talents brings a busy time that lets you thrive in an active environment. It marks the start of significant change that brings new pathways into your career. Understand that you are on a continuous growth, evolution, and change cycle. It shines a light on developing growth in your career. Essential information ahead helps you set long-term goals.

22 Wednesday

The Sun trine Pluto aspect increases your desire to gain power and drive your ambitious streak to greater heights. You have a natural knack for uncovering unique avenues that enhance your circumstances. The changes ahead bring a new growth cycle into your life. If you have felt adrift lately, you can ground your energy in a unique journey forward. Information arrives that hits a sweet note in your life.

23 Thursday

Today's Venus conjunct Jupiter aspect is a positive sign for your social life. Venus harmonizes bonds and draws a dreamy vibe when she forms a sextile with Neptune. The Venus ingress into Gemini draws balanced energy, which nurtures your romantic and social life. As Gemini adds lightness and harmony to conversations, Venus is the perfect companion which links up to growth around your tribe. Conversations are light, breezy, and fun, boosting your life.

24 Friday

Information arrives that lets you cross the threshold and enter a brighter chapter. It centers your focus on developing goals that improve your well-being and nurture your spirit. A changing scene is on the horizon, bringing a reinvigorating social aspect. It draws an active and happy chapter of engaging with the broader world of potential outside your door. It brings a windfall of abundance into your world that takes you on a journey forward.

25 Saturday

Venus trine Pluto brings an increasing drive that adds intensity as it has you focusing on developing future goals sooner rather than later. Jupiter's ingress Gemini is a favorable planetary aspect that promotes harmony. It brings fresh air into your surroundings and a light and breezy vibe that feels good for your soul. Serendipity lights the way ahead, bringing an uptick of possibility. Life ahead lines up to support your efforts to improve circumstances.

26 Sunday

Setting intentions lights a clear path forward that connects you with inspiration and creativity. Exploring leads starts a chapter of growth and planning that sees developments in your life that nurture your artistic side. Choices and decisions ahead drive expansion as an opportunity comes knocking. It brings empowering options that let you grow your world and head towards a brighter and happier chapter. It brings a windfall that moves you forward toward new possibilities.

MAY

27 Monday

You discover a journey that reminds you of your passion for life. It reconnects you with refreshing options that build a trailblazing path forward. The way ahead suddenly snaps open, bringing forward momentum toward a time of expansion. It does set off a chain of events that brings a new possibility into focus. It starts a happy chapter that brings your world celebration and joy. Changes in the air bring an enriching time that brims with potential.

28 Tuesday

With Mercury in sextile with Saturn, communication skills are rising. Enhanced clarity and mental insight help you understand more significant concepts, thought processes, and ideas with ease today. This cosmic enhancement enables you to step beyond traditional learning and take your studies/working life to the next level. Your openness and willingness to craft new goals bring a quest for knowledge, self-development, and growth.

29 Wednesday

Being open to change opens pathways that offer a gateway to a brighter future. When you are open to the potential that seeks to tempt you forward, you discover a treasure trove of options surrounding your life. It brings a journey that reveals hidden prospects and possibilities. Sifting and sorting through various options does take a degree of research, but the rewards are well worth the effort and time. It marks the beginning of a productive phase, leading to rising prospects.

30 Thursday

Mapping out ideas helps blend the energy of manifestation with your aspirations. Building stable foundations in your life is a surefire way to improve the potential possible in your world. You gently set the essence of manifestation in motion, propelling you to develop new goals. It is a golden time to explore new possibilities in your life. Breaking stagnant patterns opens your life to unique pathways that offer golden moments.

JUNE

Sun	Mon	Tue	Wed	Thu	Fri	Sat
						1
2	3	4	5	6	7	8
9	10	11	12	13	14	15
16	17	18	19	20	21	22
23	24	25	26	27	28	29
30						

New Moon

STRAWBERRY MOON

31 Friday

Mercury and Uranus form a positive aspect that heightens mental abilities. Increasing mental stimulation promotes fresh ideas in your life today. Technology, messages, and communication all spark inspiration and foster possibilities for future development. Things fall into place as new chapter ushers in a happy time for developing your talents and growing your world. It begins a highly productive journey that becomes a source of happiness and inspiration.

1 Saturday

Jupiter trine Pluto transit improves confidence and brings a powerful influence that helps you exert your power to gain control over developing your vision for future growth. You will feel more in control over the passage ahead and be able to use your mastery to obtain positive results in your life. New information forthcoming shines a light on building a bridge toward rising prospects. An area you nurture blossoms into a meaningful path worth growing.

2 Sunday

Changing priorities may shift your focus to a slower pace that promotes happiness in your life. A social aspect benefits as thoughtful discussions attract unique leads and ideas that nurture an upward trend in your life. Lively discussions with friends and companions draw a productive and engaging environment. Curious news arrives that offers insight into the path ahead. Communication arrives that opens the floodgates to socializing with friends and loved ones.

3 Monday

The Mercury sextile Neptune blends rational thinking with a dreamy aspect. It brings rising creativity and analytical thinking, promoting epiphanies that count. This cosmic alignment helps your dreams become a reality as structured backing behind your vision offers tangible results. Mercury ingress Gemini brings news and information, which adds a refreshing aspect. Communication is light and lively, adding fresh air to your surroundings.

4 Tuesday

Mercury trine Pluto attracts a questioning aspect that encourages you to dig deeper. Delving into what motivates you on a deeper level proves illuminating today. Sun conjunct Venus transit brings peaceful energy, promoting harmony, and focusing on your love relationships and personal bonds. It offers a social aspect that hits a sweet note in your life as it brings thoughtful discussions and conversations that hold meaning.

5 Wednesday

A window of opportunity is opening that helps get life on track to head towards greener pastures. Indeed, your journey ahead glimmers brightly with new possibilities. Being open to change facilitates growth and lets you take in unique pathways of learning that improve your experience. It offers a stable environment that helps you get busy and nurture your dreams. You land in an enriching landscape that fosters creativity and places the spotlight on developing plans.

6 Thursday

The New Moon offers a chance to think about the coming month and plan goals that progress life forward. Setting intentions and thinking about your future aspirations help connect with the energy of manifestation to achieve a pleasing result. You can take a deep breath and dive into the deep end as you are supported to grow your world. It helps you propel your skills forward and achieve the growth you seek in your working life.

7 Friday

Your willingness to adapt and explore new avenues of growth brings a unique path that expands your skills. You soon find the right journey to grow your abilities. Discovering pathways that take you toward growth offer soul-expanding insights and experiences. It provides a breakthrough that heralds a new chapter in your life. Feeding the fire of inspiration fuels your spirit and helps create a bridge toward a brighter future. It connects you with others who share similar abilities.

8 Saturday

You discover extra opportunities that nurture self-expression, freedom, and creativity. It brings a lovely boost as lighter energy encourages well-being and happiness. Positive sharing fosters engaging conversations that bring a connected environment. It offers food for thought as you get busy sharing with companions. It opens a path that liberates your mood with many options to explore. It lets you harness your creativity to express your abilities and advance your skills.

9 Sunday

Mars ingress Taurus focuses on long-term projects as you work slowly and methodically to achieve your goals. Exploring a variety of techniques will offer refinement and advance your skills forward. Concentrating on developing your career path enables you to gain traction on greater security in your life. It merges your aspirations with tangible results. Your patience and perseverance draw improvement into your life, offering more options to grow your life.

10 Monday

Moving beyond your current level ushers in an exciting advancement time as you climb the ladder upward. New opportunities lead to choices that grow your dreams. Evaluating options and digging below the surface of your everyday routine helps you discover choice pathways that nurture growth. Weighing up the options enables you to select the right journey that encourages your highest purpose. It imbues meaning and substance into your vision for future growth.

11 Tuesday

Mars square Pluto transit brings workplace power struggles and competition. It is a problematic planetary transit that can feel jarring. Marking clear boundaries and being specific about things does help you set appropriate barriers with someone who tends to be pushy and insistent. Keeping this person at arm's length is advisable as they can be manipulative and rude. Focusing on the building blocks secures grounded foundations that hold you in good stead as you move forward.

12 Wednesday

The wheels are moving away from outworn areas that limit progress. Fortune favors expansion, and life progresses towards an enriching time of developing unique goals. Something tempting arrives soon to breathe fresh air into your surroundings. It brings a joyous shift that helps you break free of limiting patterns. With the wind beneath your wings, you navigate with ease toward unique pathways. These changes become the building blocks to a new chapter of life.

13 Thursday

You soon make good headway around developing a fresh start in your working life. A door opens towards advancement and gives you a leg up to a prestigious area that offers rising prospects for your career path. Refining and tweaking your talents shine your skills and help you develop your working life. New choices and opportunities ahead attract excitement and spur inspiration to new levels. It lets you enter a season of growth and expansion.

14 Friday

In conjunction with Mercury, the Sun is a favorable aspect that attracts communication. An emphasis on improving your life lets you open the door to a fresh start. It sparks beautiful changes that attract curious personalities into your circle of friends. It brings a time of lively discussions and stimulating conversations with kindred spirits. Expanding your social life gets a happy chapter that ushers in new potential. It does let you make strides in expanding your horizons.

15 Saturday

A favorable aspect cracks the code to a brighter chapter. You become involved with a venture that takes on a curious light as it draws new friendships into your circle. Changes ahead bring a high note into your life. It rules a time of sharing companionship with people who get a boost into your world. Expanding your circle of friends helps you connect with others who support your personal growth and evolution.

16 Sunday

Unexpected news brings a busy time filled with the promise of a brighter future. You settle into a productive groove that grows into a meaningful path forward. Increasing freedom and adventure are on the horizon, tempting you towards lush green pastures. The seeds planted during this time blossom into a happy journey. Adding fuel to motivation sees inspiration skyrocket. It fans the flames of your creativity, allowing you to discover new pathways that nurture your capabilities.

17 Monday

Today, the Mercury square Neptune aspect can distort or make mountains of molehills. It adds a dash of illusion into your business dealings that can have your head spinning with tall tales and trying to sort the truth from exaggeration. This area is one of those days that tempt you to expand the barriers and think outside the box to develop workable solutions. Venus slips into Cancer to encourage a focus on emotional well-being and personal bonds.

18 Tuesday

The magic of possibility fuels your inspiration, and creativity rises, bringing new options to light. A path opens that represents the beginning of a journey that grows your experience. You embark on a bold chapter that offers learning, growth, and advancement. Indeed, you land in an environment ripe with potential. Being open to new pathways does grow your experience in a meaningful fashion. It paves the way forward toward change and progress.

19 Wednesday

You glimpse a compelling journey forward that offers a vibrant social aspect. Finding the missing element holds the key to future happiness. Expanding your circle of friends connects you with someone optimistic and joyful. It brings a shifting time where you focus on nurturing personal bonds. It shines an illustrious light on nurturing companionship and friendship. It brings a spontaneous time of sharing with cohorts in an engaging and relaxing environment.

20 Thursday

Today, the Neptune square Sun aspect can water down your ambitions, leaving you feeling foggy and indecisive. If your vision feels clouded, going back over your plans can help ensure they align with your vision for future growth. It takes you on a journey that brings insights into the path ahead. Evaluating all aspects allows you to cut away from areas no longer on the radar for development. Streamlining and refining your goals enables you to head toward growth.

21 Friday

A sextile between Mercury and Mars sharpens cognitive abilities today. Mental clarity is on the rise, giving you valuable insight into the path ahead. Staying flexible and adaptable helps you weather the storms and head toward advancement. Pushing back the barriers ultimately improves foundations. A transformational aspect highlights the golden opportunities ahead. Exploring unique opportunities develops your skills and grows your abilities.

22 Saturday

The Full Moon brings awareness into your spirit of the areas that seek resolution or adjustment. A time of contemplation draws clarity into the path ahead. It helps you sweep away the outworn areas that hold no future benefits. A healing and therapeutic vibe sends blessings into your world, removing the heaviness and lifting the lid on a lighter chapter. It is therapeutic for your spirit as it offers greater harmony in your world.

23 Sunday

Life-affirming endeavors capture the essence of creativity as they bring innovative options to light. It brings balance and stability into your home life. It paves the way to a chapter that offers liveliness. Little goes under your radar when you spot an opportunity to improve your life. Life holds a unique twist when information arrives, which unearths new possibilities. It clears away indecisiveness and cracks the code to a clear path forward.

24 Monday

Momentum gathers, and you redefine your life constructs by being open to advancing your skills to the next level. Working with your abilities attracts a deeper understanding of your natural strengths and skills. The conditions are ripe to extend your reach and embrace a journey that faces forward. It lets you swim upstream to new possibilities, and you soon discover smoother waters that glide you into a time of self-development.

25 Tuesday

Growing your abilities draws the knowledge to assist you with unlocking an enterprising area. Possibilities emerge that offer rising options as great potential surrounds your life. You enter a fantastic time advancing your career. Developing your skills helps you obtain growth and nail a successful outcome. You unlock a phase of new opportunities which attract rising prospects that offer prosperity. News arrives, which allows you to move forward toward advancement.

26 Wednesday

Remember to trust the path ahead as you are heading positively toward advancement. Thoughtful discussions stir a pot of manifestation that bring new ideas and options for future development. Setting your intentions and developing your goals motivates you to expand life outwardly. Being open to change underscores your willingness to adapt and grow through life. Riding a wave of hopeful energy sees you taking action to boost your circumstances.

27 Thursday

Your knack for creativity shines as you get busy and establish your gifts in an area worth your time. A buzz of excitement brings new possibilities to light that inspire learning and growth. It redefines what you thought was possible in your working life. It enables you to accomplish a great deal as it positions you in the correct alignment to climb the ladder towards a successful result for your life. Venturing into new areas develops your skills and talents in a fascinating direction.

28 Friday

Thoughtful discussions in a group environment bring rising prospects into your social life as it nurtures new ideas. It brings trailblazing and brainstorming sessions that light a path forward for your life. A new chapter lets you unpack refreshing possibilities for your social life. It offers new interests and friendships that enable you to channel your energy into growing stable foundations. It shines a light on an expressive and expansive time of engaging with a broader world of possibility.

29 Saturday

Venus's sextile with Mars draws social engagement into your life. It opens the floodgates to an enriching time that brings invitations to circulate with friends and kindred spirits. Saturn turns retrograde; this aspect focuses on the areas that hold the most significant meaning in your life. It brings a beautiful journey for nurturing your life as you move out of your comfort zone and reveal an enriching landscape of potential.

30 Sunday

Life brings a possibility into your world that is a new source of prosperity. It lets you swim upstream and discover smoother waters that offer stability and attract abundance into your life. A new chapter ahead brings beneficial changes into your life as the path clears and news arrives that gets a boost. Positive energy surrounds your social life. A changing scene on the horizon attracts the correct type of people and energy into your life, bringing an abundant landscape into view.

JULY

Sun	Mon	Tue	Wed	Thu	Fri	Sat
	1	2	3	4	5	6
7	8	9	10	11	12	13
14	15	16	17	18	19	20
21	22	23	24	25	26	27
28	29	30	31			

NEW MOON

BUCK MOON

1 Monday

Valuable rewards are on offer if you stay focused and grow your world. Information arrives that helps you build something tangible and concrete. It increases your skills and deepens your understanding of the path ahead. It leads to a busy time of gaining new skills that offer advancement. The more you explore various possibilities, the more you connect with your intuition and instincts to guide the path ahead.

2 Tuesday

Turning retrograde today, Neptune strips away illusion and any dubious realities which have clouded your vision. At the same time, the Mercury trine Neptune transit stimulates creativity and imagination and fine-tunes your instincts. Mercury ingress Leo adds an expressive vibe that enhances your storytelling and persuasive abilities. You are ready for change, and a new chapter doesn't disappoint when it offers a trailblazing path forward.

3 Wednesday

Your relationships and social bonds benefit from a steady stream of balanced energy as the Venus trine Saturn contributes loving harmony to your life. Mercury opposed Pluto increases cognitive abilities. It is the perfect transit for researching, developing business ideas, and applying an innovative approach to improving your circumstances. Trusting your gut instincts is your best bet, as you can sort through the path ahead correctly by listening to your intuition.

4 Thursday

It is a time that brings exciting news as an opportunity looms. It offers a social aspect that nurtures friendships as it gets a chance to mingle. Being open to new people and experiences marks a pleasing chapter. It brings a time of social engagement that nurtures your spirit and draws well-being into your world. It takes you to a radiant chapter that offers blessings of self-expression and creativity shared with kindred spirits.

5 Friday

Mars sextile sat Saturn adds endurance today, helping you accomplish mundane tasks and keep productive. A New Moon provides the ideal opportunity to map a plan for future growth. A window of opportunity opens, and this helps you push stumbling blocks aside and rise to the occasion as you get busy and make the most of growing your life. It provides room to progress your talents into a new area. New possibilities head to an exciting landscape that is productive and innovative.

6 Saturday

A surprise breakthrough draws new possibilities into your social life. It brings everything you need to feel happy and contented. It links with friends and brings social activities seamlessly into your world. Getting involved with attending gatherings and connecting with your broader tribe nurtures harmony and well-being. It lets you share with people who support your ideas and plans. A mix of inspiration and a lighter energy help carry you towards greener pastures.

7 Sunday

An opportunity arrives soon that brings expansion into your life. It offers a productive and dynamic environment that gets a chance to mingle with your broader circle of friends. You head towards a time that emphasizes personal growth and self-development. It aligns you with a highly creative and enterprising environment that takes you on a journey exploring new potential pathways. Life opens to a unique flavor that hits the sweet spot in your life.

8 Monday

Open-mindedness, curiosity, and a quest for adventure are prominent aspects as a Mercury sextile Jupiter alignment fosters creativity and self-expression. Information arrives soon that offers a lighter chapter. It brings a chance to dream about the possibilities as you crack the code to a brighter chapter. You head towards an active time of engaging with your social life. It brings outings and opportunities that feel spontaneous and adventurous.

9 Tuesday

you discover options that improve your world's bottom line as life offers an upswing. You land in a settled and grounded environment that sparks creative possibilities. It connects you with a journey that makes you feel optimistic about your world's prospects. Expansion ahead brings options that grow the path. You are drifting away from distractions and focusing on a meaningful journey. Being proactive kickstarts a positive trend that offers progress and success.

10 Wednesday

Welcome news brings a boost into your life. It helps you break fresh ground as you create space to nurture new goals and possibilities for your life. Movement and discovery ahead offer growth opportunities. Working with your talents and evolving your gifts is part of a more expansive journey for your life that offers advancement and refinement. It opens up a path that grows your experience and gives you a real sense of gaining traction on your goals.

11 Thursday

Venus trine Neptune transit attracts creativity, well-being, and fulfillment. Venus makes a bold statement as she gets comfy in Leo. It is a warmhearted, expressive, generous, and extravagant time. Catching up with friends nurtures well-being and places you in the correct alignment to grow your social life. Opportunities ahead bring happiness into your world. You enter an exciting time that facilitates warm expressions and heartfelt conversations.

12 Friday

Jealousy may surface as relationships face extra pressure today due to opposition between Pluto and Venus. Challenging crosscurrents can impede the flow of growth around your social bonds. Being mindful of this planetary transit helps you navigate the day with grace and thoughtfulness. Taking a moment to nurture and balance the relationships around your life draws a pleasing result worth your time.

13 Saturday

You can look forward to a refreshing change of pace. Prospects are heightening, bringing new terrain to explore. Indeed, several exciting avenues of growth light a path forward. It helps release the limitations that have blocked progress lately. It breaks up stagnant energy patterns and brings an energizing chapter to light. It brings a focus on social opportunities and gets a chance to mingle with your broader circle of friends.

14 Sunday

Focusing on expanding your social life brings a unique dynamic that offers exciting potential. Confidence heightens as you get involved with an engaging chapter of lively discussions. It nurtures a stimulating environment that sparks creative possibilities. It brings a passion project that offers a path worth growing. It speaks about news arriving which takes the edge off your stress levels. It heightens your ability to manifest possibilities.

15 Monday

Mars conjunct Uranus aspect lets you become more aware of motivations and values and discover the real reasons behind wants and desires. It provides an important clue that grows your life outwardly. Opportunity comes knocking, creating a pivotal time when you can open up your box of dreams and explore new possibilities for your life. It gets you in the mood for expansion and growth. Change and discovery unearth new leads ahead in your life.

16 Tuesday

Life moves forward with a strong emphasis on growing goals and developing your vision. A whirlwind of activity opens an opportunity that supports learning and advancement. You make an intelligent decision regarding the development of your ideas. It brings an outlet for your restless energy that nurtures your spirit and creates a secure foundation from which to grow your world. It has you moving into unique territory as you advance your skills to the next level.

17 Wednesday

You head towards an extended time that reinvents the potential possible. It speaks of a transformational aspect that has a profound effect on improving the circumstances in your world. You discover a path that offers exciting potential; it grows your world outwardly. You find options not previously encountered that bring improvements to your life. Sweeping changes are looming overhead that brings a shift forward.

18 Thursday

Opportunities to improve your working life draw stability and growth. Rising prospects open up new leads to refine your skills and develop your talents. Nurturing your abilities draws an abundant landscape that enables you to gain traction on advancing life forward. It seals the lid on a problematic chapter that feels finished. You get busy and grow your world in a unique and inspiring direction. Information ahead lights up excitement across the board.

19 Friday

You can enjoy a rip-roaring time of social growth ahead. It lets you chart a course toward developing your circle of friends and embracing new opportunities to mingle. It draws a time of lively discussions and hatching ideas with kindred spirits. It opens the door to a unique path of connection and growth. It helps break old patterns as you pick up the leads of a new journey that offers expansion. Fulfillment and happiness run rife through this brighter chapter of possibility.

20 Saturday

Mars settles into Gemini, which encourages a more diverse outlook. It helps you discover the hidden pathways and journey toward growth over the coming two months. It does help you gain traction on your career goals as it shines a light on working with your abilities and taking your talents to the next level. Climbing the ladder towards success brings a productive environment that capitalizes on your abilities to offer tangible results for your working life.

21 Sunday

The Full Moon is a chance for therapeutic healing in your life. If you face a crossroads in your life, going deeper into your goals and aspirations helps provide insight into the path ahead. You are entering a time that rules endings and transitions; it opens a new chapter that acts as a catalyst for change. Thinking about your life on a deeper level is therapeutic as it facilitates a healing influence. An area you invest time and energy into developing promotes happiness.

22 Monday

A Venus and Jupiter sextile attracts warm and abundant energy into your social life. A dash of luck and good fortune combined with enriching conversations improve social bonds in your life. Original thinking, creative brainstorming, and insightful epiphanies are the order of the day as Mercury squares off against Uranus today. Something new and inspiring flows into your life. The Sun trine Neptune alignment raises the vibration and improves circumstances in your life.

23 Tuesday

The Sun's opposition with Pluto creates a doorway through which pockets of the inner self, spirit, and primal energy can reach the surface of your awareness. It helps you make a move towards improving your home and working life. An area you become involved with developing initiates transformation. It rekindles vitality as growing creativity enables you to think outside the box and find new possibilities that bring the right platform for expressing your artistic side.

24 Wednesday

Creatively developing your talents brings stabilizing and supportive energy that improves the day-to-day aspects of your life. As you improve your circumstances, you discover an avenue worth your time. Something special makes a grand entrance and brings a transformative journey. Leaning into your strengths offers progress and growth. Indeed, exploring broader potential around your life triggers a path that nurtures growth and happiness.

25 Thursday

Mercury links up with Gemini, emphasizing connecting with your tribe. Communication and invitations flourish under this sunny aspect. Life brims with possibilities that smooth over the rough edges and promote companionship. It lifts the lid on a promising chapter of social engagement, which draws a pleasing result. It brings a fresh wave of potential into your social life, nurturing companionship and support.

26 Friday

The Sun's sextile Mars transit brings vital energy and renewed zest for life. Life turns a corner and heads towards a happy time. Setting intentions works with the essence of manifestation to crack the code to a bright time in your life. An emphasis on your social life draws a happy time as you create a path towards mingling with friends. A friendship that blossoms in your life and offers companionship and happiness.

27 Saturday

Opportunity comes knocking and brings a chapter of soul-stirring conversations shared with friends. It ushers in thoughtful discussions that balance bonds and enriches your spirit. It brings a new beginning that sweeps away negativity and ushers in change. It expands your circle of friends as a new companion pops into view, which brings lively discussions. It provides a supportive time for sharing thoughts and communication with someone insightful and wise.

28 Sunday

You are on the right path toward developing your life. It brings a time that is supportive and focuses on building stable foundations. It brings a strong focus on nurturing an emotional bond which hits a special note in your social life. Improving this tie draws opportunities that connect you with a wellspring of abundance. It lets you release stress and doubt and feel confident that your journey is evolving to a new level of potential.

AUGUST

Sun	Mon	Tue	Wed	Thu	Fri	Sat
				1	2	3
4	5	6	7	8	9	10
11	12	13	14	15	16	17
18	19	20	21	22	23	24
25	26	27	28	29	30	31

NEW MOON

STURGEON MOON

29 Monday

Today emphasizes achieving stability and growing goals in your life. It brings opportunities to grow and expand your skills as you increase possibilities by being open to enriching your life. A bustling time of expansion draws well-being as life becomes lighter and more energetic. It offers impressive results for your life. It lets you establish grounded foundations that promote a balanced environment around your life. Good luck and fortune, and support and nurture your dreams.

30 Tuesday

There are a lot of newnesses arriving to bless your life. Life brims with advanced options that open the gate to a fresh chapter. Working with your creativity offers happiness and self-improvement, guiding you toward growing your talents. Extending your reach and listening to your instincts opens a journey that grows a positive chapter in your life. Surprise news shifts your focus towards developing a unique area.

31 Wednesday

You discover a fascinating journey that deepens your knowledge and expands your skills. It connects you with kindred spirits and promotes social engagement, leading to greater happiness. A helpful influence motivates positive change in your life. It frees you to engage with life and push back the barriers. It brings various projects and plans which enhance your experience and refine your talents. You soon channel your energy into developing an area that holds meaning.

1 Thursday

As you grow your skills, you head towards a busy environment that takes your abilities to the next level. It blazes a path toward increasing the potential around your career. Nurturing your talents heightens the potential possible. A slow but steady transformation is occurring in your life. It brings fresh air that helps you move towards new goals and possibilities. It puts you in contact with others who provide supportive advice and guidance.

2 Friday

An increased need for freedom and liberation can destabilize bonds as Venus faces Uranus in a square alignment. Including your closest ties with your plans connects you with kindred spirits and helps you enjoy some well-earned downtime. Replenishing your emotional tanks restabilizes foundations as it opens the page to a new chapter in your book of life. Distancing drama and rebooting your life create foundations that harmonize and enrich your world.

3 Saturday

A sunny aspect flings open some attractive new opportunities in your life. Heightening communication attracts invitations to mingle, promoting options that ensure you are kept busy—life blossoms into an enterprising path forward that connects with refreshing companions. It sees your social circle becoming more connected, and this helps you establish grounded foundations that grow your life. It brings lively discussions and companionship to the forefront of life.

4 Sunday

The New Moon offers a chance to boost your intentions, which can assist you with working with the universe's energy to manifest your goals. An incoming assignment sparks a busy time that brings glorious developments around creativity and expression. It rules a time of expansion that helps you extend your reach and promote a new growth area. An emphasis on building stability in your home brings a happy time of evolution that holds promise for your life.

5 Monday

Venus ingress Virgo emphasizes practical matters as you build more excellent stability in your home life. A potent mix of manifestations surrounds your life as you reveal new possibilities. It connects with an upbeat time that is lively and engaging. Transformation ahead brings the chance to wipe the slate clean. It offers you a real chance at achieving growth and happiness. It triggers a journey worth your time as it lets you build a bridge to a brighter future.

6 Tuesday

Going the extra mile to nurture your dreams ensures profitability, longevity, and expansion are obtainable with a project you become involved with developing. You settle into a focused groove of setting the path ahead. It grants you inspiration and confidence; this creates the momentum necessary to progress and achieve success. Marking out a step-by-step roadmap lets you plan to achieve the best result. Focusing on the basics brings a systematic, practical approach to light.

7 Wednesday

In sextile with Jupiter, the Sun attracts a restless vibe that has you yearning to expand your life outwardly. The more you open your life to people and experiences, the more life reaches you with refreshing possibilities. Your thirst for life widens your horizons and rewards you with stimulating experiences that help you grow and prosper. It expands your circle of friends, and companionship promotes well-being and happiness.

8 Thursday

Mercury conjunct Venus brings the right time to share loving thoughts and receive positive feedback from someone who holds meaning in your life. You let your hair down and communicate openly. It brings a sense of support and connection that draws enrichment. Indeed, social events on the horizon land you in a refreshing environment. Excitement ahead nurtures growth in your social life. It brings friendship and companionship.

9 Friday

You soon open pathways that nurture a wellspring of abundance in your world. Being open to change helps the cream rise to the top as information arrives that shines a light on new goals for your life. A busy aspect brings a sense of purpose as you proactively engage with life. A whirlwind of activity overhead connects you with social possibilities. Acting on a hunch promotes a golden return that unleashes a positive trend in your life.

10 Saturday

Socializing with your friends delivers a wellspring of opportunities emphasizing a supportive vibe. It helps you build stable foundations that feel comfortable and calming. You connect with friends and companions and relish cultivating social bonds that count. As you become involved with rising potential around your social life, it charts a course towards life-affirming endeavors that renew and rejuvenate your spirit.

11 Sunday

Freedom and expansion come calling to dust off the doldrums and create sparks of creativity and potential in your life. It offers a liberating time of new adventures that sparks excitement and happiness. Being open to change creates a positive ripple effect that benefits several levels of your life. It smooths over the rough edges and promotes life-affirming endeavors and activities that speak to your soul. The essence of manifestation helps you craft plans for future growth.

12 Monday

The wheels are turning, and you soon discover possibilities promoting growth and advancement. It offers a breakthrough that sees you focusing on a big-picture goal. Lifting the shutters on an enterprising time of discovery creates a wellspring of abundance as you open the path ahead towards growth. You discover a penchant for creative areas that deepen your knowledge and expand your skill set. Investigating leads brings a refreshing cycle of expansion along.

13 Tuesday

You are approaching a crossroads when someone in your life steps forward with guidance and advice. Talking to this person is instrumental in gaining insight into the path ahead. Indeed, evaluating options lets you tap into new opportunities. Your progress towards improving your situation and touch on a promising approach that brings new projects and endeavors. It brings the right environment to launch your talents to the next level.

14 Wednesday

Today's Mars conjunct Jupiter transit is ideal for developing goals that require focused energy, initiative, and confidence. This time amplifies intuition, and you can trust your instincts to make the right decision. As you broaden the scope of what is possible, you harness creativity to achieve growth. An innovative approach takes you on a path that develops your abilities and refines your skills. It brings learning, research, and plan development.

15 Thursday

Mercury gets comfy in Leo and brings rising confidence that imbues you with persuasive abilities and an expressive spark that improves communication skills. A group enterprise with kindred spirits gets you involved with growing a journey of meaning and connection. Embracing life-affirming activities secures a stable and peaceful environment. It creates solid foundations from which to expand your world.

16 Friday

Today's aspect can feel challenging as your mind is on Saturn's to-do list. You may find it difficult to relax and unwind when your thoughts turn to the irons you have burning in the fire. Activities ahead put a spotlight on improving your life. Having the correct elements and ingredients at your disposal helps improve the prospects in your world. Good luck prominently improves fortune over the coming chapter as you get ready to launch an area that captures your interest.

17 Saturday

A new beginning shines a light on a happy and abundant landscape. It brings thoughtful discussions with family members who share new ideas. A more stable landscape emerges, which builds balanced foundations. Spending time on the home front draws a happy celebration. Something percolating in the background of your mind begins to take shape as a way forward for your life. It helps release outworn energy and get you prepared for a clean slate of potential.

18 Sunday

Original thinking, creative brainstorming, and insightful epiphanies are the order of the day as Mercury squares off against Uranus today. Something new and inspiring flows into your life. Events on the horizon beautifully support growth and expansion in your life. It offers a peek into curious pathways that nurture talents and grow your abilities. You can approach the path ahead like a tourist, sampling various options and encouraging unique adventures.

19 Monday

Independent thinking and innovative ideas are attributable to the Sun and Mercury conjunct. Today's Venus square Jupiter planetary alignment offers good things for your social life. It is the perfect time to engage with friends; lively discussions nurture creativity. Lastly, the Full Moon brings the chance to clean the slate and heal sensitive areas. Creating space to engage with a healing ritual, such as playing soft music or lighting a candle, helps nurture therapeutic influence.

20 Tuesday

You soon chart a course towards a brighter chapter and enter a growth-orientated time that brings a productive landscape into view. As you head into this time of opportunity, it takes your life towards unique areas that grow your talents. Doing research and proactively developing the path lets you immerse yourself in merging your abilities with an approach that captures inspiration. It deepens knowledge and refines skills, giving you the green light to grow your career path.

21 Wednesday

An emphasis on expansion brings a breakthrough that hits the ticket for a productive time shared with like-minded people you value. Constructive dialogues provide a thoughtful perspective that introduces new ideas and concepts. It brings a creative viewpoint that has you thinking about launching a new area. Harnessing a sense of adventure helps you initiate a way forward that takes in unique endeavors.

22 Thursday

Making time for yourself helps draw an introspective vibe which gives you insight into new pathways. Magic and creativity weave prosperous energy around your life as you move towards a fresh cycle that encourages evolution and growth. Working with your talents grows your abilities and opens the way forward. Manifesting happiness is on the agenda, and you soon crack open a time of positive change.

23 Friday

A Venus square Mars aspect can cause challenges as a difference of opinion fosters tension and conflict. Being mindful of staying flexible, understanding, and adaptive will help harmonize bonds and limit the disruption caused by Venus facing Mars at a harsh angle. Being willing to compromise will improve the foundations and limit the disruption in your life. It brings a time of letting go of areas that restrict progress.

24 Saturday

You get a chance to chill with friends when an invitation crosses your path soon. It brings an opportunity to share ideas and thoughtful discussions with kindred spirits. Indeed, relaxing and connecting with others lights a merry way forward for your social life. Meaningful moments and a touch of magic bring a comfortable and enriching environment into view. It brings practical support into your world for nurturing abundance.

25 Sunday

Your social life heats up. It brings an upward trend that offers social engagement and a chance to mingle with friends. It is an excellent time to discuss collaborations, and linking your ideas with a compatible partner allows you to join forces with someone who elevates your talents. Sharing discussions brings a percolating pot of potential, leading to designing plans for future development. A positive trend ahead gets a chance to develop progressive strategies.

26 Monday

The winds of change carry news and information into your world that offers rising prospects. It improves the foundations by bringing more balance and stability into your life. It gives you the green light to move forward and become involved with sharing with friends and companions. A carefree chapter springs to life and boosts your step as unique possibilities tempt you out and about. A situation you channel energy into blossoms into a meaningful path forward.

27 Tuesday

Exploring options will help you unearth new leads for your working life. It enables you to make a breakthrough regarding your career path. Planning the journey has you thinking about your situation in a new light. As you open a new chapter in your working life, progression shines radiantly on the horizon. A new area on offer draws dividends into your life. You build stable foundations and advance life forward by being open to embracing change.

28 Wednesday

Mercury turns direct, bringing a lighter energy flow into your social life. It improves communication and fosters improvement in relationships. It enhances communication and fosters improvement in relationships as a positive influence improves your social life and offers a happy and relaxed environment to share with your friends. Tapping into this lighter flow of potential expands your life as it lightens the load and lets you set off on new adventures.

29 Thursday

Venus settles into Libra, raising communication in your life. Personal bonds sweeten, you share ideas, and the opportunity for collaboration heightens. Today's Venus trine with Pluto adds intensity to your love life. This aspect turns up the heat in your personal life. Sexual attraction and passion rise as you get busy developing your personal life. Singles will likely find new romance soon, while couples can embrace a more connected and sizzling love life.

SEPTEMBER

Sun	Mon	Tue	Wed	Thu	Fri	Sat
1	2	3	4	5	6	7
8	9	10	11	12	13	14
15	16	17	18	19	20	21
22	23	24	25	26	27	28
29	30					

New Moon

CORN/HARVEST MOON

30 Friday

Something important will appear in your life soon. It attracts an enriching time that lines you up with unique possibilities. Positive change brings goodness to the top as you unearth new opportunities in your life. It places you in the box seat to form new friends as it widens your social circle. An invitation ahead lets you treat yourself to a relaxing and happy time shared with friends. Connecting with people you hold dear draws rejuvenation and abundance into your life.

31 Saturday

A new start flows into your life; it shines a light on a productive time that creates a strong basis for developing new goals and dreams. Creativity leads the way toward a vital shift that expands your social life and connects you with kindred spirits who nurture an abundant landscape. Sharing ideas with a tribe of creative people promotes a supportive environment. A positive ripple effect reverberates outwardly, creating waves of potential that build progressive foundations.

1 Sunday

Uranus moving into a retrograde phase boosts idealism; it offers big sky pictures that help motivate change to improve the world around you. This planetary cycle will boost your confidence and foster leadership qualities. It deepens initiative and offers a fresh wind that spurs creativity and an uptick of potential. You amplify the potential by developing solutions that propel you towards greener pastures by using your creative side.

2 Monday

Pluto gets established in Capricorn, the cardinal earth sign. This long transit is character-building. Pluto in Capricorn encourages self-development by magnifying your power and harmonizing your dreams with practical and grounded earth energies. As foundations stabilize, you unlock the gate and head towards greener pastures. It helps you move away from what has been a stormy backdrop and move towards developing an area of interest.

3 Tuesday

The New Moon offers a catalyst for change in your life. Planning the path brings stepping stones that lead to a brighter future. The Mars square Neptune aspect brings gossip and scandal to your ears. You hear surprising news that feels disconcerting. Suppose something doesn't ring true to your ears. In that case, you should do your own investigating as this transit could draw misinformation leading to confusion.

4 Wednesday

Mars ingress Cancer allows you to diversify your interests and explore new options for your life. Expanding the borders of your life sees improvement in friendship, networking, and connection. A surge of invitations arrives to connect you with others who support your life. It opens to a time filled with vibrant conversations, music, and happiness. You tap into a journey that renews and rejuvenates your spirit, leaving you optimistic about future possibilities.

5 Thursday

A lot of new energy is ready to emerge in your life. It offers a productive chapter that helps you develop new goals for your life. It brings a bold start that lets you expand life outwardly and explore new horizons that nurture creativity and abundance. It transitions you towards a journey of great promise that strengthens your life by improving your circumstances. It brings the right platform from which to express new dreams and goals.

6 Friday

A lovely perk arrives that boosts your mood as you land in an environment ripe for expansion. A shift ahead brings fundamental changes to your social life. It opens your world to new companions, and this expansion offers a liberating side to life. It lights up pathways of personal growth that help you remove any restrictive boxes that may currently limit your life's potential. It brings refreshing talks with companions, offering a more social and dynamic environment.

7 Saturday

Mercury and Uranus bring fresh ideas and epiphanies in one of the more positive square alignments. It opens a path that lets you channel your energy into an area of interest. It brings an engaging time of social interaction and friendly banter that adds playful energy into your life. It does have you dreaming big about the possibilities when you open your life to new people and experiences. It brings an active environment of mingling that offers enriching energy.

8 Sunday

The Sun's opposition to Saturn contributes to limiting beliefs, and this harsher transit can feel challenging. Focusing on the basics helps restore equilibrium. Taking it slowly today builds stable and secure foundations. It brings a boost as it draws a grounded basis from which to grow your world. Clearing away limitations lets you move forward with purpose. Lighter energy ahead triggers cascading possibilities to tempt you along.

9 Monday

Mercury slips into Virgo to raise analytical powers and provide effective solutions. You won't have to worry about competition as your work will shine above any detractors. It brings a spectacular time that has you eager to gain traction in developing your dreams. You nail a new position that offers growth and progress. It does bring collective energy that bodes well for working with others. Setting your sights on your chosen destination rings in a successful outcome ahead.

10 Tuesday

Refining your skills takes you on a comprehensive journey; it encompasses an extended time of new directions. It ultimately brings a better sense of purpose into your world. It allows you to share your talents and open your world to new possibilities that light a path toward an abundant landscape. It lets you establish your abilities in a progressive area that starts an exciting time of evolution and advancement. It offers a bright and optimistic path toward nurturing your dreams.

11 Wednesday

A fresh chapter that opens and brings rising potential that offers a sweet note of music. It energizes, reinvigorates, and brings plenty to celebrate as you get busy designing a trail that elevates prospects and advances life to a more prosperous upgrade. Creativity rises, bringing artistic and expressive elements open to a meaningful time of working with your talents to achieve a golden outcome. Helpful advice arrives to offer guidance and insight into the path ahead.

12 Thursday

A sextile between Mercury and Mars sharpens cognitive abilities today. Mental clarity is on the rise, giving you valuable insight into the path ahead. Today's Sun square Jupiter aspect raises confidence and brings good fortune swirling around your life. New possibilities crop up and provide the perfect antidote for your restlessness. It gives a chance to engage with friends, which offers a refreshing sense of connection as it renews your spirit.

13 Friday

An invitation ahead lightens the atmosphere and brings thoughtful exchanges and discussions to the forefront of your life. It helps you chart a course toward a stable and supportive landscape. It turns up the possibilities as you share with friends and forge a unique path forward that offers a wellspring of happiness. It attracts a happy time deepening ties and enjoying shared moments with friends. It connects you with kindred spirits who provide companionship.

14 Saturday

An impromptu get-together with friends attracts lively discussions and brings a strong emphasis on improving the foundations of your life. You unpack a colorful chapter that brings new possibilities. A positive change on the horizon seals the deal on a landscape of opportunity. You settle into a lively atmosphere that generates happiness. A wellspring of possibilities boosts heightened social abilities that see you get involved in a group environment.

15 Sunday

The Venus trine Jupiter aspect offers golden threads around your social and love life. It is one of the most anticipated transits which harmonizes interpersonal bonds and offers rising prospects of good luck in your romantic life. It is exciting to those seeking love or wanting a deeper romantic bond. Enjoying fun and friendship at a leisurely pace places you in the correct alignment to promote personal bonds.

16 Monday

News arrives that brings a sense of providence into your life. It opens a journey of new horizons and possibilities. It helps you launch towards a meaningful area that sparks movement and discovery. A curious path comes calling and offers to advance your skills to the next level. It forms the basis of a grounded chapter that progresses life forward. Getting involved with growing your life helps you smooth out the bumpy patches as you head towards a bright chapter.

17 Tuesday

Exploring new options draws a fresh wind into your life. It carries lighter energy that helps you create space to move in alignment with events that tempt you forward. You soon home in on new possibilities that offer growth for your life. It helps reshape goals as you head towards growth. A proactive approach draws a pleasing result. Unexpected developments ahead bring ample time for discovery. It enables you to take advantage of exciting prospects that bubble up.

18 Wednesday

The Full Moon draws a healing aspect that helps you detach and move on from outworn areas. As Mercury opposes Saturn, it brings heavy vibes into your life. Working with the energies of the Moon helps ease tension and release negativity. It's best to take things slowly and focus on the day-to-day aspects of your life. Building grounded foundations and dabbling in your hobbies offers a therapeutic influence that renews and rebuilds the foundations of your life.

19 Thursday

Today, the Sun trine Uranus aspect adds a dash of spontaneity and excitement to your life. A positive trend draws a pleasing outcome as it gets you on track to expand your circle of friends. It cultivates a more social environment that brings opportunities for collaboration. Lively discussions with kindred spirits paint a broader picture of what is possible when you link up with others with a flair for life. It opens an energizing time that draws sunny skies overhead.

20 Friday

Removing the blocks lets you get busy developing your world in a refreshing direction. Bright and cheerful energy flows into your life, harmonizing and balancing your spirit. It brings lively discussions that fuel creativity and offers inspiration. A tremendous opportunity for personal growth is on the horizon. It brings laughter and renewal to your door. It expands your circle of friends and puts you in contact with new characters who bring joy into your world.

21 Saturday

Sun-opposed Neptune adds a dreamy quality to your day, having you think about prospects. Mercury Square Jupiter adds distraction which brings a lapse of concentration. You may find it challenging to follow conversations and stay on track as your mind tends to wander under this planetary aspect. However, you can leverage this planetary transit to improve outcomes. Turning off notifications and being mindful of not engaging with distractions can enhance your focus today.

22 Sunday

Sun trine Pluto adds fuel to the creative fire burning within as it increases your desire to gain traction on long-term goals. Exploring areas that grow your world brings a remarkable turning point. It translates to a chapter that renews and rebuilds the foundations of your life. It brings a time of abundance that shines a light on possibilities that glimmer with gold. It draws an active and productive chapter of working with your abilities and growing a vision for future growth.

23 Monday

A new element enters your life soon. It brings opportunities that let you feel confident about developing new plans. As curious possibilities emerge, the tides turn in your favor. It charts a course toward change that aligns you with exciting goals that light up creativity and inspiration. Having new possibilities keeps motivation strong and helps you charge ahead toward growing your life. The right opportunity crops up that feel like the perfect fit for your life.

24 Tuesday

Laying the groundwork for expansion one brick at a time fortifies foundations and gives you a solid basis for growing your world. You connect with inspiration, giving you the green light to develop your abilities and head toward growth and learning. Nurturing your life encourages you to share your expertise with a broader audience. Developments ahead bring news and potential flowing into your life. It brings the right environment to explore advancement.

25 Wednesday

The Mercury and Neptune opposition helps you communicate your ideas and thoughts today. A dreamy influence have you talking about your vision for the future. A focus on self-development and growth provides pathways forward. It supports movement, discovery, and rising prospects. You weave pure magic by tapping into innovative options. It lets you chart a course toward a journey that fans the flames of your inspiration with new ideas and endeavors.

26 Thursday

Mercury trine Pluto offers a spiritual quality that encourages you to head towards discovery as you dig a little deeper into a personal journey. Mercury syncs up with Libra, drawing stable foundations and grounded energy into your situation. It brings news and communication into your life, harmonizing your energy and connecting with others on a similar journey. Events align beautifully to nourish your life with unique possibilities that nurture stability and well-being.

27 Friday

A refreshing change of pace draws new possibilities into your social life. News arrives, which bestows blessings as it brings a time of good fortune into your social life. It has you mingling with new people and developing a support network that nurtures lively discussions and interpersonal bonds. It brings a uniquely uplifting aspect that offers a wellspring of benefits for your spirit. Sharing thoughts and ideas with others is a soothing balm that settles your restless energy.

28 Saturday

Opportunities to engage with your friends get lively discussions and a practical sense of well-being. A social environment promotes lively discussions, bringing new options to your table. It enables a happy time of cultivating friendships that hit a sweet note. It helps you build stable foundations around your life that draw security and joy. Your ability to attract positive outcomes rises as the essence of manifestation stirs up exciting possibilities.

29 Sunday

Information arrives that grows your life experience by opening some more meaningful goals. It culminates in a shift forward that offers advancement around your life. It attracts a rich landscape of potential that sees your creativity rising under sunny skies. A new realm of options draws a rewarding result. The more you push back the barriers, the more you can connect with inspiration. Notable changes ahead highlight a journey that nurtures your life.

OCTOBER

Sun	Mon	Tue	Wed	Thu	Fri	Sat
		1	2	3	4	5
6	7	8	9	10	11	12
13	14	15	16	17	18	19
20	21	22	23	24	25	26
27	28	29	30	31		

NEW MOON

HUNTERS MOON

30 Monday

Mars trying Saturn helps you persevere and develop larger goals for your life. The Sun conjunct Mercury aspect favors communication. It brings the sharing of thoughtful dialogues and entertaining discussions. Sharing ideas with friends will help you accomplish goals and nurture well-being. An opportunity for collaboration attracts growth and a sense of kinship. You enter a cycle of increasing possibility that leaves you feeling radiant about future options.

1 Tuesday

Leaning into your strengths and pushing back the barriers help you manage the workload and head towards rising prospects. It does help you maneuver forward as you navigate a dynamic chapter. It brings more responsibilities and an upgrade to your working life. Planning a trajectory helps usher in innovative options that align with growing your talents. News arrives to get a boost into your life. It brings a time of developing leads and mapping out a strategy for future contingencies.

2 Wednesday

The New Moon brings fresh energy and a sense of wonder last. Being open to developing new ventures brings a sense of purpose and happiness to your life. It is the ideal time to find a new way to move forward constructively in your life. Relishing a new project brings research and planning; it raises the vibration around your life. Investing time in developing viable leads drives a renewed sense of purpose. It enables you to strike gold and advance toward a rich landscape.

3 Thursday

Careful thought and planning grow the path ahead and carry a positive aspect fuelled by your positive approach to life. Rising prospects heighten creativity, enabling you to deepen your knowledge and advance your skills. It lights up pathways of increasing possibilities that help you turn a corner and head toward lucrative options. You discover a venture that captures the essence of inspiration, enabling you to forge new projects.

4 Friday

Today's Venus trine Saturn transit is ideal for developing relationships. Self-expression, warmth, and affection flow freely under this favorable aspect. It marks a time of social engagement and sharing thoughtful discussions with others who understand your take on life. Having the proper support in your world nurtures happiness and joy. Expansion around your circle of friends attracts companionship and thoughtful discussions.

5 Saturday

A freedom-loving vibe encourages growth and expansion. It brings new people into your inner circle, and lively discussions uplift and nurture your life with new possibilities. So much to look forward to, as lighter energy brings a refreshing time that promotes social engagement. Networking and getting involved with get-togethers get a boost to morale. New ideas crop up for possible future development.

6 Sunday

Mercury Square Mars is a harsh alignment that can see disagreements bubble to the surface—thinking before acting can be a saving grace. "Fools dare where angels fear to tread" is an old proverb that speaks volumes about this planetary transit. Pausing to evaluate before acting or speaking on an impulse will serve you well today. Biting your tongue and saving harsh words may be the best action to prevent issues in your social bonds under this short-lived planetary aspect.

7 Monday

Life heads towards an upswing ahead, which starts a fresh growth cycle. It helps you make strides in improving your world. You can redefine the path forward and make the most of the possibilities that seek to emerge in your life. Clearing the blocks helps establish stable foundations. The seeds you plant blossom into a thriving chapter. It starts a lively and productive chapter that offers a whirlwind of new possibilities. It brings a phase of liberation, freedom, and expansion.

8 Tuesday

Venus trine Mars raises your energy and brings a boost to your life. News arrives, which brings a snap decision. It opens the floodgates to an enriching time that brings invitations to circulate with friends and kindred spirits. It offers a beautiful adventure that nurtures your social life and helps you reach a destination that inspires your world. It draws a stable foundation and brings an active phase of lively conversations and opportunities to mingle.

9 Wednesday

Jupiter turns retrograde, emphasizing spiritual growth and getting in touch with what truly moves you on a soul level. It helps you sweep away all that stands in the way of developing your goals. Embracing your higher potential lets, you release the heaviness and embrace a fresh start. You soon get a taste of moving out of your comfort zone and exploring options that tempt you toward growth. In terms of manifestation, your creative abilities and mental focus are heightening.

10 Thursday

Some positive news is looming overhead. Discussions ahead bring a thoughtful vibe into your life. It releases stress and lets you flick anxiety to the curb. It enables you to get involved with an area that offers room to grow. Collaborating with others brings an extended time that gives you the green light to get involved with new endeavors. News ahead lights an exciting path forward. It brings a curious new lead that offers room to advance life forward.

11 Friday

Your social life picks up steam and opens a journey of adventure and excitement. It offers a curious change that brings improvement as it expands your circle of friends. A quickening of pace links to a social environment that is enriching and lively. It focuses on developing companionship, and close talks with others lift the lid on enterprising options worth your time. Innovative solutions and sharing life with others bring a supportive environment.

12 Saturday

Pluto turns direct, bringing an appropriate time to re-evaluate your life. Pluto rules transformation and brings hidden insights to the surface of your awareness when in a moving forward phase. Nurturing your dreams opens the path for your life. It does lay the groundwork sustainably to grow your situation and develop plans that progress life towards advancement. You enter a landscape of green and lush possibilities, and creativity rises to meet new challenges.

13 Sunday

Today's aspect causes a challenging environment as you find your judgment or authority tested. Being challenged and tested feels uncomfortable as you think you are making the right choices and decisions for your life. The Mercury square Pluto transit also attracts interactions with other people who feed the gossip mill and cultivate drama, leading to a toxic environment. Mercury cozies up to Scorpio, bringing a probing and questioning aspect that has you wanting to reveal the truth.

14 Monday

The Sun forms a trine with Jupiter, which increases good luck and fortune in your life. You open pathways that nurture personal growth and cultivate abundance in your social life. It does bring a full life circle as you reconnect with someone from your past. A social aspect ahead brings harmony and lively engagement into view. It offers a bustling time of sharing with friends and engaging in thoughtful discussions as you find your groove in a more social landscape.

15 Tuesday

Expect intensity as the Sun square Mars alignment may leave you feeling restless. Venus opposed Uranus's alignment bringing growth to personal relationships. Increasing synergy and chemistry could spark a new romance or flirtation opportunity. It paves the way toward growing unique bonds that promote happiness. It brings a busy time that emphasizes building security and improving bonds in your social life. It generates a time of lively discussions and opportunities.

16 Wednesday

Venus trine Neptune transit attracts creativity, well-being, and fulfillment. You are going through a time of transition. New options emerge that shift your focus to developing unique goals which hold meaning. You enter a phase of evolution that continues a more comprehensive theme of improving circumstances. Creativity rises, bringing new possibilities to light that offer a way forward. It brings a group environment that connects you with like-minded people.

17 Thursday

The Full Moon helps you turn a corner as you reveal lunar healing, which empowers your life with renewal. It brings a new approach that revitalizes your spirit. You soon lift the lid on an expansive journey that heightens prospects in your life. It brings a blossoming time of chasing your dreams and developing remarkable goals. It promotes enrichment and progression as Venus settles into Sagittarius, bringing an uplifting, buoyant and optimistic influence.

18 Friday

Rising prospects help you create a bridge towards a brighter chapter that marks the start of growing your world in a unique direction. Curiosity leads you towards a little worn path that offers growth and refinement of talents. Getting involved with working with your abilities draws a pleasing result. Transformation ahead grows the happiness in your life. Blazing a trail towards increasing your skills marks the start of something big.

19 Saturday

Surprise news ahead lights the path forward. It brings a new chapter with plenty of lively activity to shine a light on nurturing your soul. Taking down the filters of what is possible releases the limitations and blocks. It dissolves outworn areas as plenty of lightness ramps up inspiration and potential in your world. It brings new creative projects that connect you with like-minded people. Getting in touch with forgotten hobbies and talents brings inspiring projects to your life's forefront.

20 Sunday

A growing theme of improving your life supports expansion in your world. It translates into a new journey where you share the lessons learned from the past with others who may benefit from the insight you have gained. Indeed, a stable landscape emerges that nourishes your life as you embark on a bold chapter of embracing life-affirming endeavors. The way forward is bright and optimistic as new options that support artistic expression arrive.

21 Monday

Leveraging your skills to obtain advancement draws rising prospects. Innovative techniques combined with your intuitive intelligence help you gain traction in achieving your chosen objective. It does bring a time of designing the way forward, and as you mark out the stepping stones, you discover new ideas that increase motivation and creativity. Your dedication to growing your world draws a pleasing outcome.

22 Tuesday

Mercury trine Saturn adds endurance and gives you extra fuel in your tank to achieve heightened productivity today. The Sun square Pluto aspect draws renewal and rejuvenation. Pluto charts a course toward transformation and offers a highly creative part that lights the way forward toward improving your circumstances. The Sun contributes to golden beams that offer harmony, transcendence, and rising prospects.

23 Wednesday

Maintaining excellence draws growth as you receive opportunities that increase your career's potential. It does bring heightened security and a pleasing result to your working goals. A lovely perk arrives, a feather in your cap that has you re-evaluating your working life goals. It offers ample time for growth and rising prospects. It marks a chapter that puts your talents front and center. Being open to advancement helps catapult you to the next level in your career.

24 Thursday

You open a new path that brings unique experiences and opportunities into your career. A creative assignment on the horizon teams you up with others who support you. Getting involved with areas that promote your growth and evolution will help you continue to evolve and prosper. News arrives, which brings a boost to your spirit. Your working life is headed towards expansion as rising prospects get into a busy and dynamic environment.

25 Friday

Mars sextile Uranus brings unique ideas that help you think outside the box to obtain innovative solutions. Uranus places the focus on rebellion, liberation, and freedom. It adds a dash of spontaneity to your life today. A surge of new possibilities stirs up a sense of excitement. News reaches you that unlocks a gateway towards future growth. Life is active and busy, letting you initiate developing goals.

26 Saturday

Embracing new possibilities offers a path that brings a journey worth growing. Sharing with friends and loved ones nurture well-being and cultivate rising creativity. Options pop up to support growing your world, and this openness you express takes you in a direction that draws abundance. The tides turn in your favor and bring lively discussions and social opportunities your way. You secure balanced foundations in a warm and lavish landscape.

27 Sunday

A social aspect ahead brings refreshing potential into your world. An invitation to mingle nurtures well-being and offers thoughtful discussions with your broader circle of friends. Bright and cheerful energy flows into your life, harmonizing and balancing your spirit. It provides a chance to nurture grounded foundations and draw stability into your home life. It brings a radiant aspect that offers a lively and dynamic portal to a brighter chapter.

28 Monday

Under the influence of a Mars and Neptune trine, creativity soars, and epiphanies and lightbulb moments are the order of the day. Exploring thoughts and ideas takes your imagination to impressive heights. It teams you up with a joint project that offers collaboration, networking, and communication. Weeding out distractions lets you focus on nurturing the potential possible. As you paint the backdrop of your vision for growth, you discover room to extend your abilities.

29 Tuesday

A bold new beginning in your life marks a pivotal time where you can spread your wings and head towards rising aspects. A swift decision initiates waves of transformation that heighten the potential possible. The outlook ahead is rosy with luck and luxury, offering better security and stability. A side project taps into your artistic inclinations, and leaning into this area provides room to nurture harmony and well-being.

30 Wednesday

The Mercury opposed Uranus' transit bringing a chaotic and hectic pace. The busier pace may leave you feeling tense, anxious, and scattered. Uranus adds a dash of the unexpected, leaving you scrambling to deal with surprise news. Information emerges from the blue, leaving you wondering what will happen next. Focusing on the basics improves balance; if you are feeling pressure today, take a moment to breathe and relax.

31 Thursday

You can wipe the slate clean and link with a fresh chapter of potential. A therapeutic quality offers healing benefits to wash away old spirit wounds. If emotions feel sensitive, remember you can attract positive outcomes by releasing the past and renewing your energy. Being selective helps you spot a diamond in the rough that brings an area worth your time.

November

Sun	Mon	Tue	Wed	Thu	Fri	Sat
					1	2
3	4	5	6	7	8	9
10	11	12	13	14	15	16
17	18	19	20	21	22	23
24	25	26	27	28	29	30

New Moon

BEAVER MOON

1 Friday

Creativity, imagination, and innovation blaze a wildfire of inspiration as Mercury and Neptune form a trine today. Increased sensitivity to this vibrational energy attracts a boost into your world that bolsters vitality. It offers a dramatic shift that helps you quickly learn or develop a new area. Making intelligent choices leads to a breakthrough. It does encourage advancement as you head towards growth. You can harness the New Moon's energy today to start something new.

2 Saturday

A Mercury trine Mars aspect attracts a restless vibe. This cosmic alignment leaves you feeling spontaneous and ready for new adventures today. It links you to a path that brings gifts and luck. It captures the essence of wanderlust and offers an exciting journey forward. A creative aspect helps bring artistic expression out in the open. An expressive and trailblazing time following your heart begins a positive trend that expands your life.

3 Sunday

Mars opposing Pluto brings a drive to succeed and gain traction on growing your long-term goals. Venus opposes Jupiter and brings good fortune into your romantic life. It adds an indulgent vibration and has you wanting to explore hedonism, romance, and magic. It brings positive prospects that open the way to a busy and exciting time that redefines what is possible in your life. Beautiful changes ahead give you the green light to focus on developing personal goals.

4 Monday

Mars ingress Leo raises confidence and helps you go boldly into uncharted territory to achieve growth in your life. Additionally, today's Sun trine, Saturn, offers constructive dialogues that enhance your creativity and stimulate new pathways of possibility. It brings changes, and as refreshing options pour in, you discover one that offers outstanding prospects. It brings the right environment for artistic expression, and a creative undertaking is soon a strong focus in your life.

5 Tuesday

News ahead signals a changing landscape that helps give you a leg up on a more stable and prosperous environment. Keeping open to new possibilities encourages developing goals that align with your creativity and talents. New opportunities sweep in to promote renewal. It brings a bright and beautiful time that lights up a sunny destination. It brings harmony into your life as your creativity sparks new possibilities. It marks the beginning of an enriching journey forward.

6 Wednesday

Exploring options draws a fresh wind of possibilities. It helps you navigate a complex environment and develop solutions that offer a fresh start. It brings choices that lead to a breakthrough. You uncover confidential information that draws clarity and insight into your life. New information ahead creates a positive shift forward for your life. Expect signs and serendipity that tempt you to try new avenues.

7 Thursday

A new possibility springs to life soon. Discussing the potential possible with friends leaves you feeling energized and excited about developing this area. Investigating unique options brings a cycle of steady growth to your door. It has you working smarter, not more complexly, as you use creativity to develop innovative solutions. A glittering opportunity ahead brings a busy and active shift toward new adventures.

8 Friday

A creative assignment on the horizon teams you up with others who support you. Getting involved with areas that promote your growth and evolution will help you continue to evolve and prosper. News arrives, which brings a boost to your spirit. It liberates your mood with a freedom-loving environment that captures the essence of adventure. Manifestation gently weaves magic through your life by restoring well-being and promoting harmony in your world.

9 Saturday

Life becomes more socially connected and enriching as you expand your horizons and link up with others with similar interests. It offers notable changes that highlight a journey that promotes a busy and lively time of social inclusion as you mingle with friends who nurture happiness. Changes in the air align with a slow but steady transformation that improves foundations. As events unfold, you bring an enriching chapter to light that sees emotional well-being soaring.

10 Sunday

A social aspect brings a journey that advances life towards a wellspring of potential. It gets a lovely boost as you foster developing personal bonds that lead to companionship. Greener pastures beckon and tempt you forward. Lively discussions get insightful ideas and the opportunity to spend more time with your crew of friends. Connecting with your broader circle brings companionship. Information arrives that cracks the code to the chapter ahead.

11 Monday

Venus ingress Capricorn draws grounded energy that has you feeling capable of developing stable foundations in your life. A social aspect draws soul-expanding conversations and entertaining dialogues. It provides an abundant chapter that nurtures your spirit by drawing well-being into your surroundings. A sense of social connection directs your attention to sharing and rekindling the magic in your world.

12 Tuesday

A block may prevent you from achieving peak performance today as Mercury square Saturn creates challenges around communication and sharing free-flowing ideas. You can set boundaries with people who leave you feeling drained. Conserving your emotional energy leaves you feeling more empowered and ready to tackle new projects and endeavors. Set tangible limits on areas that distract your focus. Channeling energy with a laser beam focus improves prospects today.

13 Wednesday

Weeding out areas that failed to come to fruition help you make room for more relevant projects. You are in your element when developing an endeavor that inspires you creatively. Being adaptable and open to change helps you advance your talents into a unique area that expands your life. Research and planning are valuable tools to unearth the right leads. Progressing your plans forward helps ground your energy in a journey that cultivates well-being.

14 Thursday

Being flexible and open to whatever the world presents helps you make the most of the potential that arrives. You open a path that brings unique experiences and opportunities into your career. Learning and growing enable you to assess your strengths and lean into advancement. Being productive promotes bright optimism that grows your life outwardly. Essential changes flow into your life, drawing happiness and inspiration. You make waves as you get busy developing dreams.

15 Friday

Saturn turns direct, lifting the shutters on an enterprising chapter that sees forward propulsion moving you towards beneficial outcomes for your life. The Full Moon draws a therapeutic influence that reboots your energy and wipes sensitive areas from your spirit. Scheduling outworn areas for deletion brings a focus on improving circumstances that boost your spiritual, mental, and psychological well-being.

16 Saturday

Inspiring news comes out of the blue. It is a welcome remedy as an invitation to mingle brings a big plus to your social life. It offers a more socially connected phase that nurtures well-being and happiness. New inspiration grows magic around your creativity during this engaging time. A lot of good comes into your life as a social aspect spins news and opportunities. Confidence rises, seeing your personality sparkle in a group environment.

17 Sunday

The Sun-opposed Uranus transit attracts a restless vibe that gives you the green light to try something new and different. It drives a liberating chapter that offers spontaneity as you get busy expressing your unique melody and personality. As you chart a course toward exploring new leads, a sense of wanderlust guides your vision. You find your feet in a landscape ripe for progression. It helps initiate a positive chapter that carries you forward.

18 Monday

Today, Mercury opposed Jupiter draws a favorable aspect that nurtures good fortune in your social life. A time of transformation snags a lighter chapter that offers social engagement and community involvement. It launches a time of promoting stable foundations as you get busy with new projects on the home front. Building sound foundations ushers a fruitful time to link with your circle of friends.

19 Tuesday

Being proactive helps you spot meaningful career leads that generate rising prospects. A positive change takes your vision further. A pathway opens, bringing an influx of opportunity. You stake your claim in an ambitious area that captures the essence of excitement. It makes you feel optimistic about possibilities, giving you the green light. Advancing your skills become a strong focus as you climb the ladder toward success.

20 Wednesday

Putting the shine on your talents promotes genuine advancement and creates space for new goals to emerge. It marks a journey in which significant change is possible. A compelling journey ahead draws remarkable results. It lets you gain traction in developing your dreams. It corresponds with planning, gathering intel, and having all the resources required to advance life. Watch for signs as important clues reveal unique opportunities meant for your life.

21 Thursday

Today's Sun sextile Pluto transit drives ambitions and sees you with an increased drive to succeed and conquer your goals. It lets you progress and expand your horizons into areas that deepen your knowledge and grow your abilities. New possibilities raise confidence and bring a newfound energy to develop projects of meaning. It ignites a passion for working with your skills and increasing life outwardly.

22 Friday

Today, Venus sextile Saturn promotes cooperation and offers the chance to join a joint project. The curious changes ahead offer a compelling journey forward for your life. Indeed, it soon becomes a gateway from which to grow your world. You tap into a journey that brings a stimulating social environment that facilitates developing new areas. Lively conversations fuel expansion in your circle, bringing a trail of happiness to tempt you forward.

23 Saturday

A gateway opens that gives you a joyous journey to channel your energy into development. A catalyst for change helps you discover those areas that offer the most incredible abundance in your world. Your willingness to be open to all possibilities draws a bountiful selection of options into your world. An idea takes shape and crystallizes into a meaningful path forward for your life. It encourages you to take the plunge and dive into new territory that expands your horizons.

24 Sunday

A charge of positive energy moves into your home life, bringing unprecedented options for growth and expansion. It offers to revolutionize the potential around your life. It brings social gatherings and events to mix with family and friends. Sharing ideas and fascinating conversations with kindred spirits provides ample time to increase your life's stability. It lets you cross the threshold and enter a lighter and happier landscape of possibility.

25 Monday

Surprise developments ahead improve the security in your life. It lights up avenues of success and prosperity as you turn the corner and head towards lucrative options worth your time. Learning and growing enable you to assess your strengths and lean into advancement. Weeding out areas that failed to come to fruition help you make room for more relevant projects. You are in your element when developing an endeavor that inspires you creatively.

26 Tuesday

Mercury turns retrograde, which creates a challenging environment for growing personal bonds. Miscommunication is more prevalent during this planetary cycle, leading to communication blocks and misunderstandings in your love life. Understanding the tailspin Mercury retrograde does on your social and love life helps you be more mindful during a planetary phase of challenging crosscurrents and miscommunication.

27 Wednesday

Sun trine Mars raises creativity and highlights positive energy around your thought processes. Rising possibilities influence your life by increasing good luck. A sense of fate brings an enticing invitation that opens a magnificent time shared with friends. Feeling happy and sharing moments with friends and family brings a spectacular time for designing unique goals which hold meaning and potential for your life. It places you in a solid alignment to improve circumstances.

28 Thursday

A lucky break opens in your social life. It brings an invitation that fuels inspiration and leads to a busy time where you can focus on improving the building blocks of your foundations. Having a solid basis from which to grow your dreams brings an emphasis on developing life and nurturing your goals. Home and family life becomes a sound focus that encourages happiness and promotes growth. Being productive promotes bright optimism that grows your life outwardly.

December

Sun	Mon	Tue	Wed	Thu	Fri	Sat
1	2	3	4	5	6	7
8	9	10	11	12	13	14
15	16	17	18	19	20	21
22	23	24	25	26	27	28
29	30	31				

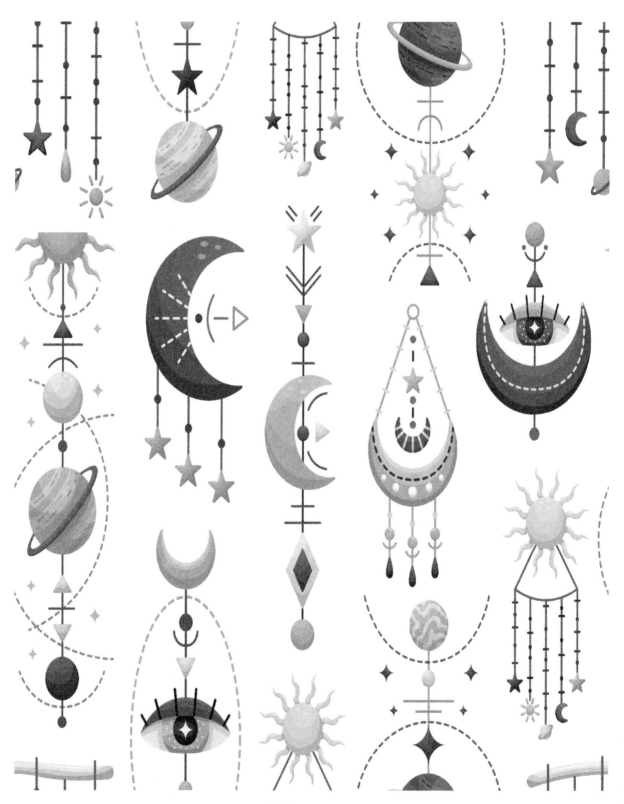

New Moon

COLD MOON

29 Friday

You will enjoy the magic and happiness ahead as it raises the vibration around your life and promotes harmony with your circle. News arrives that points you in the right direction to connect with friends. It brings moments to treasure and a chance to sync with others. Cherish the moments and enjoy a fun time catching up with others around your life as it builds stable foundations which promote a pleasing outcome.

30 Saturday

Your love life heads on an upswing and deepens a bond that promotes romance and magic for your love life. It brings fun catching up and moments to treasure. Messages and communication are free-flowing, with heartfelt stirrings that foster emotional depth. It brings a gorgeous time to enjoy all that life has to offer as you discover romantic threads of abundance around your life. Deepening a bond and engaging in the dance of love brings happiness.

1 Sunday

The December New Moon brings an empowering aspect as new opportunities arise, boosting your support networks. Information and developments help nurture a unique perspective and outlook on life. It shows a more socially active environment. It brings news that hits a high note and draws sunshine overhead. As you transition onward, you discover expansion blooms around your life, bringing important communication to your door.

2 Monday

A Venus trine Uranus aspect adds a dash of spontaneity and fun to your life. It speaks of goodness rising to the top this holiday season. Your social life pops like firecrackers as many invitations, communications, and news emerge to promote happiness and festivity. Dazzling opportunities enable an upward trend that brings a bumper crop of possibilities. Mingling and networking improve life and draw happiness and well-being as you discover an uptick in your social life hits the spot.

3 Tuesday

It is a busy time that promotes a productive pace. It is a good time for establishing your talents and achieving growth, security, and progression. Leaning into the added demands on your time helps you lead with your strengths. It is a fluid and changing environment that brings challenges and potential. Working with your abilities enables you to shine as those above take notice of your adequate and efficient track record.

4 Wednesday

Mercury-opposed to Jupiter brings positive communication and news. Saturn is the ruler of honoring traditions. Today's square with the Sun illuminates a happy time shared with loved ones, perfect with Saturn, who delights in celebrating established bonds. Venus sextile with Neptune sends loving beams into your home and family life, harmonizing bonds and drawing the essence of rejuvenation and renewal to your door. She builds grounded and stable energy around your life.

5 Thursday

Change is in the air as you soon unpack rising potential for your social life that draws expansion and happiness. Indeed, someone reaches out with confidential news, which delivers a wellspring of joy in your life that lightens the load on your shoulders. It attracts a rich landscape of potential that sees your confidence rising under sunny skies. It brings a lively adventure to your social life that draws a burst of inspiration into your world.

6 Friday

Mars retrograde offers a chance to remove hidden blocks that prevent progress from occurring in your life. It is the appropriate time to confront aspects you usually repress. Now is the time to dig deep and look at any unresolved conflicts limiting your true potential. Reevaluating your life offers a new outlook that marks a turning point. You refuel energy tanks and head off towards setting new goals that inspire your mind.

7 Saturday

Venus ingress Aquarius brings a desire to connect with people who resonate on your wavelength. Venus, the ruler of love, offers an abundant landscape when conjunct with Pluto. The energy of transformation surrounds your life, enabling you to advance your romantic life. Manifesting your happiness is on the agenda as you deepen your romance aspirations and grow the potential possible in your love life. You begin to see what is possible when you expand the borders of life.

8 Sunday

Venus opposed Mars, increasing drive, chemistry, and sexual attraction. It connects with a lively crew who draw fresh energy into your life. Hitting the town with kindred spirits brings special moments and festivities that promote advancement for your love life. A lively exchange emphasizes improvement and this sense of connection leaves you feeling optimistic about future potential. It brings a wave of hopeful energy toward rising prospects.

9 Monday

Acting on instincts lets, you embark on a progressive phase that gains momentum and draws an active time of working with your talents. It is a time that draws change and brings an option that advances your situation forward. A new adventure comes calling and blossoms into an exciting path forward. As you navigate the stepping stones toward success, it sets the tone for an inspiring time of chasing your vision

10 Tuesday

A new possibility creates a stir of excitement. It reveals information that lets you plot a course toward developing a curious venture. It bestows blessings and opens life to new pathways. A time of heightening creativity and expansion enables you to tackle an ambitious project. Life becomes busy, giving you the proper nourishment to spread your wings and map out new goals. As you create the stepping stones forward, you maintain stable foundations and draw security.

11 Wednesday

Some news is coming that brings excitement; it removes limiting beliefs around security. It opens the floodgates to an enterprising avenue forward. It brings an active and productive chapter of working towards your vision. It gets a chance to branch out and grow your talents. Dramatic change ahead improves your environment as prize news looms overhead. It draws an opportunity that lets you climb the ladder toward success.

12 Thursday

Working in an assembled group brings harmony and happiness. It engenders positive feelings as you enjoy a more connected environment around your social life. Putting your talents center stage elevates potential and sparks increasing options that promote security. It encourages expansion and culminates in an upgrade to your situation. An emphasis on designing goals brings exciting plans ahead.

13 Friday

Today's Mercury sextile Venus adds a positive influence that harmonizes and nurtures well-being in your world. Less stress and more enjoyment grow solid foundations. Personal relationships benefit from open communication leading to fulfillment. Things change for the better and bring an optimistic vibe ahead. An invitation to connect with friends attracts an enriching environment. People reach out to sync up with you. It brings social engagement and a lively atmosphere.

14 Saturday

Your social life reigns supreme as you discover new opportunities to mingle and make friends. It has you eager to be part of the celebrations and festivities as your circle of friends broadens with a spontaneous flair for adventure. Sharing ideas and thoughts with others heightens creative abilities and brings exciting options to the forefront of your life. A sudden opportunity emerges that feels like the right fit.

15 Sunday

A glorious Full Moon helps you turn a corner. It signals a chance to heal the past and go beyond what you thought was possible. It can bring out strong emotions, and finding therapeutic ways to channel these sensitive feelings positively draws healing. Mercury turns direct, which releases negativity around personal and social bonds. Any crosswires during the retrograde phase will soon lift as lighter energy attracts a positive influence in your life.

16 Monday

You come into your own as you discover pathways that open life to a new and unique flavor. It brings opportunities to dabble in interests and refine your talents. Life goes your way as good fortune emerges, bringing happiness as you design dreams and work on growing your life. A sunny destination supports growth as you deepen your knowledge and advance your goals. It brings a glittering time that takes your abilities to the next level.

17 Tuesday

This month is a beautiful time to design and plan future growth opportunities. Imagination and creativity are rising, enabling you to access pathways that offer progress and growth. You benefit from expansion, and working with your abilities draws advancement. You hit the Jackpot and discover an enterprising time offering fortune and favor. Refining your gifts cracks the code to a bright chapter. You enter a busy time that brings refinement, progression, and advancement.

18 Wednesday

You can prioritize your goals and achieve a robust result when you put your mind to developing your dreams. You channel your energy into a pathway that promotes greater happiness. Designing plans for next year sees you working steadily to achieve progress around your vision for future growth. It opens life up to a social environment that expands your circle of friends. New faces, thoughtful discussions, and invitations to mingle blaze a trail forward.

19 Thursday

You enter a time of transition that can feel unsettling; it brings memories as you revisit the past and contemplate treasured moments. You face a crossroads, but information emerges to connect you with others who bring support and fresh energy. Expanding your social life brings inspiration and news, which restores balance. An invitation to mingle initiates lively discussions and a sense of celebration that sparks festivities.

20 Friday

Good news will flow into your life soon. Life picks up momentum and brings social opportunities you can treasure. It has you feeling connected and more in tune with developing happiness. An invitation ahead hits the high note that brings a celebration to your life. It offers an expansive and optimistic time for sharing thoughts and connecting with friends. It provides a therapeutic landscape that allows you to create a brighter path.

21 Saturday

Adventure comes calling and links you to a social environment. You receive an invitation that captures the essence of wanderlust and adventure. An expressive and trailblazing time of sharing thoughtful discussions begins a positive trend that expands your social life outwardly. It unleashes a lively environment that brings a chance to mingle with friends. Nurturing personal bonds promotes happiness and well-being.

22 Sunday

Open-hearted discussions pave the way forward toward improving social bonds. You draw harmony and deepen ties within your circle. A lively and engaging time of sharing thoughtful discussions supports a time of growth. This Christmas is a time of memories and revisiting the past as a sentimental theme flows into your life. Designing and thinking about the future does help you cross the threshold and enter a brighter chapter filled with possibility.

23 Monday

Opportunities ahead draw a happy chapter for your home life. It brings a celebration that lets you dive into a time of fun and liveliness. You discover a page-turning environment brings fresh energy around your social life. It drives a phase of wanderlust as new opportunities crop up, which promote expansion. The more you push back the boundaries, the more you discover life blossoms. Linking with friends creates stable foundations that promote happiness and well-being.

24 Tuesday

The Jupiter square Saturn aspect signifies overspending could bring a crimp to your finances. If you feel a little blue about financial prospects, creating a budget and planning to repay the credit cards in time will help you balance your money woes. However, as the year draws to a close, you unwrap a time of endless possibilities that tempts you to plan and design the journey ahead. It triggers a time that offers discovery, change, and opportunity for your life.

25 Wednesday

Christmas Day. Life showers a double dose of goodness over your situation. It brings a social aspect that entertains in a lively and vibrant atmosphere. A sense of celebration hangs in the air as you get busy catching up with friends and loved ones. Lively discussions draw clear skies overhead as you reach a new understanding of your life. This happy event brings joy. You settle into a vibrant environment and share warm conversations with family and friends.

26 Thursday

Today, Mercury is the show's star and draws a favorable aspect that nurtures good fortune in your social life. It brings a chance to share with friends and loved ones. Relaxing and unwinding enable you to restore frazzled nerves and build robust foundations. You enter a time of inspiration, manifestation, and engagement with friends. A more social aspect brings a breath of fresh air into your surroundings. It gives a boost to confidence and increases happiness.

27 Friday

Mercury square Saturn challenges social talks. Tensions could flare up and lead to disruptions. Miscommunication is more likely when you are not on the same page as the person you are talking to about your thoughts and ideas. Focusing on open and transparent communication can help you be on the same wavelength during this challenging aspect. Taking a moment to soothe frazzled or sensitive emotions draws a pleasing outcome today.

28 Saturday

You may notice a sentimental vibe that brings a softness into your life. Poetic and insightful energy creates a cocoon around your soul. Devoting time to dabbling in your hobbies and connecting with friends and family sees you feel content and secure. Focusing on the priorities this holiday season brings happiness and harmony to your door. You settle into a happy time filled with warmth and joy. News on the horizon gets a lift as it promotes a heartening social aspect.

29 Sunday

You can expect developments around your social life to bring a fresh wave of possibility which offers excitement and joy. It lets you breathe fresh air into your surroundings as you feel renewed and embrace positive change. A new cycle begins, shifting your focus forward; it connects with others who offer thoughtful discussions. Sharing thoughts and ideas heightens the potential around your life and brings new possibilities into focus.

30 Monday

An exciting destination comes into focus. It leads to a time filled with growth, happiness, and fulfillment. You create a ripple effect that opens life outwardly and brings far-ranging benefits. You open a social environment that helps you stay connected with friends and family. Mingling and sharing words with others with similar values bring a richly creative focus which is perfect for exploring new ideas.

31 Tuesday

You open a journey that takes you to an emotionally abundant chapter. It does rejuvenate your personal life as you deepen a romantic bond that lights up pathways of growth and inspiration. It brings romance and magic into your life. A sense of synchronicity and serendipity tells of blessings and a meaningful journey in your life. It lights the way forward that promotes happiness and harmony.

1 Wednesday

More abundant energy flows into your private life. Invitations, communication, and news keep you on your toes as your romantic life hums along, bringing remarkable progress which offers transformation. It grows a journey that nurtures a wellspring of abundance and magic in your world. The influence of this growth echoes around your life, bringing happiness, optimism, and joy. You can design new goals that tap into avenues that enrich and reward.

2 Thursday

Life brims with possibility as you chart a course toward development. Negotiating advancement brings a focus on growing life outwardly. It seals the deal to improving your life. Rising motivation attracts inspiration and confidence that helps you gain traction on your goals. You gain access to a prosperous environment that is key to future growth. You touch down on a landscape ripe with opportunity. It triggers a cascade of new options for your life.

Astrology, Tarot & Horoscope Books.

Mystic Cat

Printed in Great Britain
by Amazon